Police Ir̶̶̶̶̶

Recruitment

Test

Mock Test

(WITH PREPARATION)

C J Tyreman

ELC Publications

Second Edition
Copyright © 2001 ELC Publications

Published by ELC Publications
PO Box 91, Bangor, North Wales, UK, LL33 0ZF

British Library Cataloguing in Publication Data
A CIP record for this book is available from the British Library.
ISBN 0953864634

Printed and bound by Antony Rowe Ltd, Eastbourne

Part 1 – Basic English Skills

Part 1

<u>BASIC ENGLISH SKILLS</u>

(For the Police Initial Recruitment Test -PIRT)

First Published 1998
Second Edition
Copyright © 2001 ELC Publications

Contents

THE POLICE ENTRANCE TESTS

INTRODUCTION

THE recruiting procedure for the Police Force varies slightly from one Force to another. However, to gain entry, you must:-

➢ be over age 18 years of age (21 for some Forces),
➢ be of British Nationality (or a Commonwealth citizen with un-restricted stay in this country),
➢ pass an interview
➢ pass the Police Initial Recruitment test (PIR test)
➢ pass a medical
➢ pass a physical fitness test

Height/Weight

There are no longer any height or weight restrictions, however, you must be in proportion! To give you some idea, you can work out your Body Mass Index (BMI). This is given by your height in centimetres, divided by your body weight in kilograms once, and then again.

BMI = height in centimetres ÷ body mass (kg) ÷ body mass (kg)

Example: John weighs 75.5 kg and is 1.84 m tall.
John's BMI = $75.5 \div 1.84 \div 1.84 = 22.3$

A BMI value of:
20 to 25 is suggested as normal / healthy
26 to 30 is overweight
over 30 is obese
less than 19 is underweight

Eyesight

Exact requirements vary from one Force to another. If you wear vision aids, your optician can carry out an aided/unaided vision check (Snellen's test) and colour vision check.

Physical Fitness

Lack of physical fitness is probably the biggest reason why most people are turned down.

Regular exercise is essential if you are to achieve the necessary level of fitness. The exercise you do should be of an *aerobic nature*, to improve the heart and circulatory system. You must possess good cardio-vascular fitness.

Aerobic fitness can be improved with aerobics classes; circuit training; running; swimming; football; racket-sports, dancing etc. Weight training is not as effective. The aim is to breathe more deeply and to improve the heart and lungs. Smoking is detrimental to cardio-vascular fitness

By way of example, all applicants for Greater Manchester Police are required to pass 'circuit training' type tests. These include sit-ups, press-ups, burpees and, in addition, a twenty metre shuttle at an ever increasing pace. Regular practise is essential if your are to achieve the required standard in these tests.

This page has been deliberately left blank

The PIR Test

THIS course will help you to pass the Police Initial Recruitment test which is taken by all people wanting to enter the police force (with the exception of university graduates).

There are five separate tests which make up the test battery. They use 'multiple-choice' type questions and answers. You choose the correct answer from those given.

Police officers have to deal with a wide variety of situations and require skills in all five test areas.

TEST 1 - Verbal Usage
This test requires the correct usage of words. It checks your English grammar and spelling skills.

TEST 2 - Checking Information
This test requires 'proof-reading' skills. You check through information as quickly as possible, looking for text errors.

TEST 3 - Working with Numbers
Mathematics – don't worry! – the mathematical skills are very basic and consist of 'number type' problems. Be careful though, you cannot use a calculator for these questions.

TEST 4 - Verbal Reasoning
These questions require reasoning skills and logical thinking. You sift key facts from information supplied, that is to say, simple deduction and problem solving.

TEST 5 - Memory Skills
Police officers must be on the alert for anything and everything. This test involves the accurate observation and recollection of life-like scenes. Would you make a good witness? What is your memory like?

Test 5 uses a video presentation. As such, it is beyond the scope of this course, however, we have included visual material that will help you to prepare for this test.

Speed is essential throughout the PIR test battery. All five tests are individually timed on a strict basis. This course contains exercises with time limits. Try to complete each exercise within the allotted time wherever possible.

Good luck.

This page has been deliberately left blank

Basic English Skills

TEST 1 - VERBAL USAGE

TEST 1 in the entrance test battery checks your word skills and in particular your spelling and grammar.

Aspects of Grammar
Verbs ("doing" words)

Verbs are a very important part of writing and speech because they are "doing" words. This means that verbs tell you what is happening or what action is taking place. Examples of verbs in their simplest form are:

> to throw
> to laugh
> to work
> to think
> to run

A verb we often use is "to be", in the form of "is", "are" and "am".

These are used in:-

> I am
> you are
> he is
> she is
> it is
> we are
> you are
> they are

He, she and it, go with is.
We they and you, go with are.

So: he is late, they are early.

They is late, we is early, <u>are both wrong.</u>

Now try the following 'In-Text Question' (ITQ).

ITQ 1

Find the verb in each of the following sentences and write it in the box provided.

1. He hit it with his baton. `hit`

2. You drive the car home. `drive`

3. I drink tea in the afternoon. `drink`

4. Open the door for me. `Open`

5. We are at the top. `locate`

6. I am late today. `am`

7. He is in front of you. `is`

8. It is ready now. `is`

Singular and Plural Verbs

To make most verbs plural, all you need to do is add an "s" to the end.

So: throw becomes throws
    sing becomes sings
    laugh becomes laughs
    run becomes runs   etc.

"I", "we", "they" and "you" use the singular verbs (throw, sing, laugh, run). "He", "she" and "it" use the plural verbs (throws, sings, laughs, runs).

5

So: I run, we run, they run, you run, but: he runs, she runs, it runs.

Similarly:
I go, we go, they go, you go,
he goes, she goes, it goes.

Notice that we add "es" to the end of the verb "go" to make it plural.

ITQ 2

Complete the following with the correct verb (singular or plural). The first verb is shown in each case.

1. I speak /we _speak_ /they _speak_
   it _speaks_

2. She laughs/they _laugh_ /you _laugh_

3. He writes/they _write_ /you _write_
   John and I _write_

Nouns

A noun is the <u>name</u> of a person, place or thing, and is often the subject of the sentence. The subject is the thing we are talking or writing about. Examples of nouns are given below:

Person	Place	Thing
baker	town	car
optician	city	television
salesman	village	potato
boy	park	piano
girl	cinema	knife
son	station	coat
brother	room	dog
lady	office	pen

Proper Nouns

These are nouns that begin with a capital letter. They include names of people, countries, businesses, roads and streets, days of the week and months of the year, people with a title and titles of books, films and poems.

Names of people, countries, months days, roads etc.	People with a title (positions held)	Titles of books, films, plays etc.
John	Prime Minister	Treasure Island
Tom Cruise	Doctor Watson	David Copperfield
Australia	Chancellor Khol	Psycho
Tuesday	President Clinton	Neighbours
Ramsay Street	Captain Philips	Othello
December	Professor Einstein	Titanic
Sainsbury's	Princess Di.	Les Miserables
British Airways	Inspector Clouseau	Goldfinger

ITQ 3

Underline the nouns and proper nouns in the sentences below. The verbs have been written in **bold ink.**

1. The boy **runs** quickly.

2. We **walk** to the shops.

3. The Prime Minister will **speak** on Monday.

4. Our Prime Minister **is** Tony Blair.

6. I **read** the morning newspaper.

7. I **eat** my meal with chopsticks and a spoon.

8. Bob can **speak**, English, French and German.

6

Collective Nouns

These are nouns that denote many individuals. They use the singular verb. In the examples below, the collective noun is written in **bold** ink and the singular verb is written in *italics*.

The **choir** *is* singing (not 'are' singing).

The **jury** *has* decided. (not 'have' decided').

The **government** *was* in session. (not 'were' in session).

Other collective nouns include:-
army, audience, class, club, crowd, committee, congregation, flock, gang, group, herd, swarm, team.

Adjectives

An adjective describes a noun and tells you more about it. Adjectives are placed in front of nouns. Examples of adjectives are given below. They are <u>underlined</u>. The noun comes after the adjective and is written in **bold ink** in these examples.

The <u>young</u> **boy** runs quickly.
We walk to the <u>local</u> **park**.
The <u>clever</u> **Prime Minster** speaks <u>next</u> **Monday**.
I read an <u>interesting</u> **book**.
I eat my <u>hot</u> **meal** with <u>two</u> **chopsticks** and a <u>single</u> **spoon**.
Bob speaks <u>excellent</u> **English**, <u>good</u> **French** and a <u>little</u> **German**.

Subject and Object

In a sentence, the words are grouped together in an order that the person reading can understand. All sentences MUST start with a capital letter and end with a full stop. They always contain a verb ("doing" word) in the middle.

A sentence begins with a *subject*, which is often a person or place (i.e. a noun). A sentence is often finished by adding an *object*. The object is the person or thing (a noun) at which the action (verb) is aimed. Not all sentences have an object, but they all have a subject. To give the sentence more meaning, the last noun is often joined to another noun to complete the picture. For example:

The waiter serves the customers
  (object) (verb)   *(object)*
with cold   drinks.
  (adjective) (noun)

Past and Present Tense

Verbs are used often in the present tense when spoken. The past tense shows that the action took place at an earlier time. When we write, we often use the past tense. Many past tense verbs can be made from the present tense by adding the letters "ed", (and sometimes making slight spelling changes). These verbs are known as "regular verbs" and examples are given below.

Present tense verb	Past tense verb
walk	walked
joke	joked
play	played
mend	mended
smile	smiled

7

If the sentence contain two verbs, then we have to change the tense of both verbs if we change the tense of the sentence. For example:-
Present Tense
She is late and so misses her train.
Passed Tense
She was late and so missed her train.

Some of the verbs we often use have an "irregular" past tense. Examples are:- (past/present tense)

am/was	are/were	is/was
(I)	(you,we,they)	(he,she,it)

eat/ate   do/did   draw/drew
drink/drank   flies/flew   freeze/froze
forget/forgot   go/went   get/got
choose/chose   give/gave   have/had
know/knew   hear/heard   tell/told
leave/left   make/made   say/so
ride/rode   sing/sang   shake/shook
swim/swam   write/wrote

ITQ 4

Which one is grammatically correct?
1.
A . I am ready if you is.   O
B. I is ready if you are.   O
C. I'm ready if you is.   O
D. I am ready if you are.   ⊘

2.
A . We is happy if she is.   O
B. We are happy if she are.   O
C. We are happy if she is.   ⊘
D. We are happy if she are.   O

3.
A . We was ill after he was.   O
B. We were ill after he were.   O
C. We was ill after he were.   O
D. We were ill after he was.   ⊘

4.
A . It was faster than he was.   ⊘
B. It were faster than he was.   O
C. It were faster than he were.   O
D. It was faster than he were.   O

5.
A. Either you is right or I is.   O
B. Either you is right or I am.   O
C. Either you are right or I is.   O
D. Either you are right or I am.   ⊘

6.
A . I were late and left alone.   O
B. I was late and leave alone.   O
C. I am late and leave alone.   O
D. I am late and left alone.   ⊘

7.
A. It was you who were last.   O
B. It were you who were last.   O
C. It was you who is last.   O
D. It was you who was last.   ⊘

It is important that you have answered all seven questions correctly. If you have made a mistake then you should go back and read the text again.

Adverbs
We have discussed adjectives - words which describe nouns, earlier in the course. Now we must think about words which describe verbs. These words are called adverbs; they are usually placed after the verb, and tell us more about it.

The adverbs in the following sentences are underlined and the verbs are in bold type. Notice how many adverbs end in "ly".

8

Janet **arrived** early.
He **ran** quickly.
Trevor **shouts** loudly.
John **drives** carelessly along the road.
We **work** hard.
Ian **writes** carefully and neatly.

Some adverbs tell you when an action (a verb) is taking place. For example: today, yesterday, soon, immediately, before, now. Note that these adverbs (underlined) do not always follow the verb (**bold type**).

They **rang** yesterday.
She **comes** today.
He **went** before me.
He soon **left** the party.
I immediately **phoned** the police.

You have seen how many adverbs end in "ly" and may have realised that these adverbs are formed from adjectives (- remember adjectives describe nouns), simply by adding "ly". For example:

The quiet boy crept quietly out of the room.

Personal Pronouns

These are used in place of nouns. Sometimes it becomes boring to use the same noun all the time, for example:

"Peter dove the car. Peter crashed the car. Peter was taken to hospital."

In the second and third sentences, we might replace the nouns "Peter" and "car" with pronouns. The pronouns are underlined:-

"Peter drove the car. He crashed it. He was taken to hospital."

There are seven pronouns. They have different forms depending whether they are used to replace the *subject* or the *object*, except for "it" and "you" which are the same in both cases.

	SUBJECT	**OBJECT**
1.	I (NOT i)	me
2.	you	you
3.	he	him
4.	she	her
5.	we	us
6.	they	them
7.	it	it

Here are some sentences showing how pronouns may be used to replace nouns:-

Peter went to see Paul.
replace with: He went to see him.

Peter went to see Paula.
replace with: He went to see her.

Jane caught Richard and Susan.
replace with: She caught them.

John and David came early.
replace with: They came early.

Robert and I ate the food.
replace with: We ate it.

9

ITQ 5

Re-write the following sentences, replacing the underlined words with pronouns. The first question has been done for you.

(Hint: replace the underlined word(s) at the beginning of the sentence with a pronoun from the "subject" list in the box opposite; replace the underlined word(s) at the end of the sentence with a pronoun from the "object" list in the box opposite.)

1. Sarah wrote a letter.

----She wrote it -----

2. Frank closed the door.

he closed it

3. Geoff met Julie.

he met her

4. Pam made dinner for John.

She made it for him

5. Ian and Mike posted the letters.

They posted them

6. Helen and Tim came to see my friend and me.

They came to see us

ITQ 6

In the following sentences, write on the dotted line the correct personal pronoun from the choice given above the line. Refer to the table on the previous page if you are unsure which pronoun to choose. The first question has been done for you.

I/me   she/her
1. I listened to the music with **her.**
    subject   object
                    I/me
2. Richard and __I__ are friends.
        s u b j e c t   object
                                    I/me
3. Richard can go with you and __Me__.
        subject   o b j e c t

    They/Them   we/us
4. __They__ ran towards __us__.
        subject   object
                    I/me
5. You and __I__ will leave together.
        s u b j e c t
                                    I/me
6. His father is taller than __Me__ , but
            subject   object

we/us   they/them
__We__ are taller than __them__.
subject   object

The personal pronoun always has the subjective case when it follows the verb *to be* (as in *it is, it was, it were,* etc.) Spoken English sounds stilted with the subjective case so the objective case is often used in speech, however, it is incorrect when writing.

10

ITQ 7

Insert the correct pronouns, all of which follow the verb *to be*.

he/him

1. *It was* __him__ *I saw at the house.*

   subject

she/her

2. I think *it is* __her__ *leaving now.*

   subject

they/them

3. *It was* __them__ *all along.*

   subject

I/me

4. *It was not* __me__ *but it could*

   subject

he/him

be __him__.

subject

Comparatives

Earlier we learned that adjectives are used to describe nouns. These adjectives are known as *positives*. We can also use adjectives to compare nouns, in which case the adjectives are known as *comparatives*. When we compare two nouns we use a *superlative*.

For example: John is <u>taller</u> than Bill. John, Bill and Ken are tall, but Ken is the <u>tallest</u>.

Notice that the comparatives change from "taller" to "tallest" when we go from comparing two nouns to comparing three nouns.

Comparing nouns:

Adjective (positive)	Comparative (2 nouns)	Superlative (3 or more)
tall	taller	tallest
brave	braver	bravest
hard	harder	hardest
small	smaller	smallest

Usually we add "er" and "est" to make the two different comparatives, but there are exceptions. These are well known and are given below.

Adjective (positive)	Comparative (2 nouns)	Superlative (3 or more)
good	better	best
many/much	more	most
little	less	least
bad	worse	worst

ITQ 8

Complete the following sentences by putting in the correct comparative or superlative. The positive adjective is given in each case.

1. brave: Jim is __braver__ than Dick.
2. hard: This work is _____ than the last.
3. easy: This work is _____ than the last.
4. large: Your room is _____ than mine.
5. bad: Of all three, your writing is the _____.
6. many: I have _____ money than my husband.
7. good: David's work is good, but comparing his with Barry's, Barry's is the _____ of the two.
8. good: John's work is good and so is Julie's but Dawn's is the _____.

(spelling hint question 3: change "y" to "i")

11

The Apostrophe

The apostrophe is probably the most misused mark of punctuation in written work. Most mistakes are made because apostrophes are used when they are not needed. The most common error is to insert an apostrophe with an ordinary plural noun, for example:

There are six book's on the shelf. - THIS IS WRONG.

There are six books on the shelf. - THIS IS CORRECT.

The apostrophe has two uses. The main use is in "possession" and the other use is in "contractions". We will look at each in turn

Possession

Here, the apostrophe is used to show that something belongs to the owner. We add 's to the end of the owner's name. Examples are shown below. Notice that the owners are singular - this means that there is only one owner.

Jim's hat (meaning the hat belonging to Jim).
Dad's car (meaning the car belonging to Dad).
The lady's gloves (meaning the gloves belonging to the lady).

If there is more than one owner (the owner is plural) then we add ' to the end of the owner's name. Examples are shown below.

The players' ball (meaning the ball belonging to the players).
The Jones' dog (meaning the dog belonging to the Jones).

The girls' babies (meaning the babies belong to the girl).

Notice that the plural owners (nouns), shown above, all end with an s, (players, Jones, girls). If the owners do not end in an s then you need to add 's to the end of the owners. Examples of plural nouns not ending in s are: men, children, sheep, fish. Examples of adding 's to the end of plural nouns not ending in s are:

The children's school (the school of the children); the policemen's helmets; the women's clothing.

ITQ 9

Make the sentences possessive using the apostrophe.
The owners are singular:
1. The spade belonging to Tom.
_____Tom's spade_____
2. The cows of the farmer.

----

3. The sons of my neighbour.

The owners are plural:
4. The noise of the animals.

----

5. The sails of the yachts.

===========================

Plural owners which do not end in s:
6. The boots of the men.

----

7. The boat of the fishermen.

12

Contractions

When speaking we often "cut down" or contract words to make a short version. When writing this short version an apostrophe mark is placed above the position of the missing letter or letters, and the two words involved are bunched together.

"did not" becomes *didn't*
"could not" becomes *couldn't*
"have not" becomes *haven't* -
- missing 'o'.
"he is" and "he has become *he's*
"it is" and "it has" become *it's*
- missing 'i' and missing 'ha'.
they will" becomes *they'll*
- missing wi

-The second word loses a letter(s) and the <u>first word remains unchanged</u>.

ITQ 10

Write the short form.

1. he is   __he's__

2. that is   _____

3. I am   _____

4. they are   _____

5. we will   _____

6. they will   _____

7. there is   _____

8. we have   _____

9. who is / who has   _____

ITQ 11

Write these short forms <u>in full</u>. Questions 5, 6, 8, 9 and 10 have two possible answers, one of which is given.

1. doesn't   _____

2. weren't   _____

3. haven't   _____

4. we're   _____

5. when's __when was__ or _____

6. I'd __I should __ or _____

7. can't   _____

8. it's __it was__ or _____

9. we'll __we shall__ or _____

10. I'll __I shall__ or _____

Quotation Marks

Quotation marks, sometimes called speech marks or inverted commas, written "_____" (or sometimes '_____') are used to indicate actual words spoken by someone. This means when direct speech is used.

Examples of direct speech often occur in novels. Here are two examples:

"You've been a long time coming," said Bond.
"Sit down," Felix said.

Notice that the comma is placed between the actual words spoken and the remainder of the sentence. The comma should be <u>inside</u> the quotation marks.

13

If the sentence is written a different way, the comma goes <u>before</u> the quotation marks and the first word of the direct speech starts with a capital letter, as shown below:

Bond said, "You've been a long time coming."
Felix said, "Sit down."

Note that any number of sentences can be included inside the direct speech. There in no need to close the quotation marks and start new ones. Now study the three examples:

1. Felix frowned. "Sorry, I can't allow that. You cannot break the speed limit."

2. "Room service?" said Bond. "Please send me a bottle of vodka and one of Martini. You can put them on my bill."

3. "I hit him over the head," said Bond, "and I think he's dead."

Example 3 shows the correct use of the comma both inside the quotation marks and before the quotation marks, as described earlier. Use this example to help you to answer the following ITQ.

ITQ 12

Put speech marks in the sentences and add commas where necessary. The first question has been done.

1. "Come inside this minute," shouted the boy's mother.

2. That's very kind of you he said cheerfully.

3. My brother said I can't make it.

4. Good morning said Mr Evans. I am pleased with your progress. You must have a pay rise.

5. I must go said Mary because I am meeting my husband shortly.

6. I hit the ball over the boundary said Boycott and no one can find it.

7. Hey you boy! he yelled. Come here. I'm fed up with your mis-behaviour.   (Hint: see example 3)

Future Tense
Will
The future tense tells us what is going to take place in the future. To express the future we use the verb "will". For example: I will be late home tonight.

The verb in the above sentence is "will be". It is made from the two verbs "will" and "be" because "will" cannot be used on its own. Examples are:-
I <u>will take</u> you home later.
They <u>will arrive</u> tomorrow.
You will catch a cold.
We <u>will try</u> harder next time.

Sometimes "will" becomes separated from the other verb in the sentence. Examples are:
I <u>will</u> not <u>take</u> you home.
What time <u>will</u> they <u>arrive</u>?
<u>Will</u> it <u>be</u> the same?

Will may also be combined with two other verbs to complete the verb in the sentence. For example:

Canadian wheat <u>will be bought</u> by the Government in greater quantity than last year.

Would

"Would" is normally used instead of "will" if we want to express the future from some time in the past. So for example:

I think I will go home tomorrow.
 (now)
I thought I would go home today.
 (earlier)

Shall and Should

These are weaker alternatives to will and shall. For example:-

I shall attend the lesson, says that you intend to attend at some future date, but *I will attend the lesson*, states that you are definitely going to turn up. If you are unsure about whether to use will or shall, then <u>use will</u>, since although it may not be the best choice, it is never wrong.

Should is a weaker alternative to would in some sentences and it is better to use should with verbs of "liking" as this often sounds more polite. So for example:
I should like to come, is more polite than *I would like to come*.

Participles

These are verbs with modified endings. They are frequently used in written work and speech because they show continuous action. There are two types of participle.

1. Participles describing continuous action.

These are the "ing" form of the verb. Examples are walking, running, playing, drawing, thinking, trying, drinking, etc. These "ing" forms are often more useful than the simple tenses (past, present and future) because they describe continuous action. They are combined with all three tenses (past, present and future) to give the complete verb for the sentence, which then tells you what is happening, what was happening or will be happening. Examples are given below (participle in italics; sentence verb underlined).

I <u>am washing</u> the dishes.
I <u>was washing</u> the dishes.
I <u>will be washing</u> the dishes.
You <u>are writing</u> a letter.
You <u>were writing</u> a letter
You <u>will be writing</u> a letter.

2. Participles describing completed action.

These are normally called *past participles* and describe completed action. They are used with all three tenses (past, present and future) and show that the action is finished, has finished, or will be finished. Examples are given here (past participle in italics; sentence verb underlined):

I <u>have *washed*</u> the car.
I <u>had *washed*</u> the car.
I <u>will have *washed*</u> the car.
You <u>had *written*</u> a letter.
You <u>will have *written*</u> a letter.

15

Many past particles can be made by adding "ed" to the end of verbs. However, many past participles end in other letters as shown on the next page. The present tense of the verb and the past tense of the verb have been included for comparison with the past participle (p.p.).

Present tense	Past tense	p.p. (past partciple)
am	was	been
begin	began	begun
blow	blew	blown
break	broke	broken
choose	chose	chosen
do	did	done
drink	drank	drunk
eat	ate	eaten
forget	forgot	forgotten
freeze	froze	frozen
give	gave	given
go	went	gone
have/has	had	had
know	knew	known
leave	lost	lost
ride	rode	ridden
sell	sold	sold
shake	shook	shaken
sing	sang	sung
tear	tore	torn
throw	threw	thrown

ITQ 13

Complete the following sentences by choosing either the first verb (past tense) or the second verb (past participle). Hint: the past participle can be used with all three tenses (past, present and future) but is often used with "had".

1. By the time the sun had _____
rose/risen

the climber had _____ to ascend
began/begun
the summit.

2. He had _____ away the purse
threw/thrown

that he had previously _____
stole/stolen

3. The post was collected just before

I had _____ my note and _____
wrote/written   ate/eaten

my lunch.

4. We _____ our beer before we
drank/drunk

_____ home.
went/gone

5. We _____ down on our seats
sank/sunk

after we had ---------- home.
run/ran

6. I haven't _____ a car before.
drove/driven

7. The lock will have _____
froze/frozen

SPELLING

AT the simplest level, the police test will check your knowledge of words which sound the same but are spelt differently and have a different meaning. These words are known as homophones (or homonyms). Some examples are given below.

their (meaning belonging to)
e.g. They ate their dinner.
there (meaning a place)
e.g. Put the book over there.
right (a direction, or correct)
write (script)
to (with verbs/nouns/ pronouns)
two (meaning the number two)
too (meaning more than enough, also or as well)

> *ascent* and *assent*
> *been* and *bean*
> *course* and *coarse*
> *deuce* and *juice*
> *dough* and *doe*
> *hare* and *hair*
> *piece* and *peace*
> *shoot* and *chute*
> *scene* and *seen*
> *stair* and *stare*
> *way* and *weigh*

The following pairs words are not homophones, however, they can give trouble:

enquire - ask / *inquire* - investigate

enquiry - question / *inquiry* - official investigation

ensure - make sure / *insure* - take out insurance

Now try the following in-text question (ITQ) to check your knowledge of homophones. Keep to the allotted time.

ITQ 14

Pencil-in the circle under the correct answer. Pass mark = 5 correct answers in 1 minute.

1. _____ was no place to hide.
   There   Their
   O   O
2. The theft was _____ to see.
   plane   plain
   O   O
3. She spoke the _____ truth.
   whole   hole
   O   O
4. Do not _____ your time.
   waist   waste
   O   O
5. He fell _____ the ceiling.
   threw   through
   O   O
6. They would _____ first.
   practise   practice
   O   O
7. He held no driving _____.
   licence   license
   O   O
8. Police were called to the _____.
   seen   scene
   O   O

17

Spelling Rules

Words are built using *vowels* and *consonants* from the alphabet. There are five vowels: a e i o u The remaining letters of the alphabet are consonants.

Every word in the English language must contain at least one vowel, except short words such as my and by where y takes the place of the vowel i.

A *syllable* is part of a word that has one vowel sound, often with consonants. For example:

show - one syllable
vowel - two syllables
pronunciation - four syllables

There are few fixed rules for spelling, however, you may find the following guidelines helpful.

1. Most candidates will be familiar with the rule 'i before e except after c'. This holds good for nearly all words in which the vowel-sound is ee:

i before e:
believe; diesel; field; hygiene; piece; shield; siege; tier; yield;
except after c:
ceiling; conceit; conceive; deceive; deceit; perceive; receipt; receive.

Exceptions to 'i before e except after c' include: caffeine; either; counterfeit; forfeit; heinous; inveigle; neither; protein; seize; weird and species.

2. Many candidates are unsure how to add suffixes to a root word. Suffixes include: -ed, -en, -er, -ery, -est, -ing, -less, -ly.

When the root word ends in e, the e is usually dropped if the suffix begins with a vowel but is retained if the suffix begins with a consonant:

hope   hopeless   hoping (no e)
use   useful   usable (no e)
bribe bribery   bribable (no e)
care   careless   caring (no e)

However, the e is retained in words ending -ce, -ee,-ge and -le. Peace / peaceable, agree / agreeable, bridge / bridgeable, sale / saleable, mile / mileage. Other exceptions are: argue / argument, true / truly, due / duly, whole / wholly.

3. Words ending in y and preceeded by a consonant, change the y to an i when adding the suffixes -ed , -er or -able. For example: carry / carried / carrier and deny / denied / deniable.

However, the y is retained when preceded by a vowel or when adding -ing. So: enjoy / enjoyable / enjoying, convey / conveyed / conveying.

4. Full becomes ful when added to the end of a root word: beautiful, helpful, useful, joyful, mouthful, wilful, skilful, grateful, spoonful. The above adjectives ending in ful, add the ending -ly when made into adverbs:

The beautiful day ended beautifully.
The skilful player played skilfully.

5. When the suffix -ly is added to a word ending in y the y changes to an

18

i, for example: necessary/ necessarily, happy / happily. Exception: shyly

6. When the suffix -ly is added to a word ending in a consonant + le, change the e to a y, e.g. able/ably, terrible/terribly.

7. When the suffix -ing is added to words that end in -ie, the e is dropped and the i becomes y, for example: die/dying, lie/lying.

8. When adding mis- or dis- to the beginning of a word, there is only one s unless the root word begins with s. agree / disagree, appear / disappear heard / misheard, spell / misspell

9. When adding un- or -in at the beginning of a word there is only one n unless the word itself begins with n. usual / unusual/, destructible / indestructible, necessary / unnecessary

10. When adding suffixes to short words of one syllable the last letter of the root word is often doubled, as shown by beg / begged, hit / hitting, sad/sadden.

Doubling of the last consonant also applies to words of two syllables if the word is stressed on the last syllable as with begin / beginner, occur / occurrence, rev / revving, befit / befitted - but not if the word isn't stressed on the last syllable as in offer / offering.

Exceptions are kidnap / kidnapped and worship / worshipping.

Words which end with more than one consonant do not double the last letter: bald / balding, halt / halting.

11. Words ending in the letter l double the l even if the stress does not fall on the last syllable. So: jewel / jewellery, control / controllable, travel / traveller. Exceptions are: parallel /paralleled, appeal / appealing If the suffix does not begin with a vowel, then the final consonant is not doubled: enrol / enrolment, annul / annulment, rival / rivalry.

12. The consonants h,w,x and y are never doubled.

ITQ 15

Choose the correctly spelt (spelled) word from the four alternatives. Fill in the circles that go with your answers. Move on to the next question if you get stuck. The questions continue over the page. You have 15 minutes to answer 60 questions. Pass mark = 40 correct answers.

	A	B	C	D
1.	acheave O	achieve O	acheive O	achiev O
2.	bellieved O	believed O	beleaved O	beleived O
3.	repreave O	reprieved O	repreived O	repriev O
4.	decieve O	deceave O	deceive O	deceeve O
5.	reciept O	receapt O	receipt O	receet O
6.	siesure O	seizure O	siezure O	seezure O
7.	neighbor O	neighbour O	nieghbour O	nieghbor O
8.	beseage O	beseige O	besiege O	beaseige O
9.	hight O	hieght O	height O	hite O
10.	frend O	freind O	frende O	friend O
11.	insureance O	innsurance O	insurance O	innsurrance O
12.	raceism O	racisem O	racism O	racizm O
13.	sensable O	senseble O	sensible O	sensibel O
14.	chargible O	chargeable O	chargabel O	chargable O
15.	enforcebel O	enforceable O	enforcable O	enforceible O
16.	noticable O	noticeable O	notissable O	noticeabel O
17.	agreeible O	agreeable O	agreeble O	agreable O

20

	A	**B**	**C**	**D**
18.	succesfull O	sucessful O	successfull O	successful O
19.	unlawfull O	unnlawfull O	unlawfull O	unlawful O
20.	waistful O	wastefull O	waistfull O	wasteful O
21.	beggining O	begginning O	beginning O	begining O
22	refering O	reffering O	referring O	refferring O
23.	occurrance O	occurance O	occurrence O	occurence O
24.	referance O	refference O	reference O	referrence O
25.	appearrance O	apearance O	appearance O	apearrance O
26.	livelyhood O	livleyhood O	livelihood O	liveleyhood O
27.	coppies O	copys O	copies O	copyies O
28.	lying O	lieing O	lyeing O	liying O
29.	dying O	dieing O	diying O	dieying O
30.	ocasionally O	occasionally O	ocassionaly O	ocasionaly O
31.	immediatly O	immediately O	imediately O	imediatly O
32.	disscretely O	discretely O	descretely O	discretly O
33.	huriedely O	hurriedly O	hurriedely O	hurriedly O
34.	sinserely O	sincerely O	sincerly O	sinserely O
35.	enrollment O	enrolment O	enrolement O	ennrolment O
36.	transfered O	transferred O	tranceferred O	trancefered O
37.	unnecessary O	uneccesary O	unnecesary O	unnessesary O
38.	possession O	posession O	posesion O	possesion O

	A	B	C	D
	A	**B**	**C**	**D**
39.	addresses O	addresess O	addreses O	adresses O
40.	embarrassed O	embarased O	embarased O	embarrassed O
41.	Britan O	Brittan O	britain O	Britain O
42.	collige O	colege O	college O	colledge O
43.	procedure O	proceedure O	proseedure O	prosedure O
44.	convenient O	conveneient O	convienient O	conveniant O
45.	anonymous O	annonymous O	anonimous O	annonimous O
46.	casuallty O	casualtly O	casualty O	cassualty O
47.	bisness O	businness O	busness O	business O
48.	vanderlism O	vandalism O	vandallism O	vanderllism O
49.	surveylance O	surveillance O	surveyllance O	surveilance O
50.	commited O	committed O	committed O	comitted O
51.	benefited O	benefitted O	bennefitted O	bennefited O
52.	govenment O	government O	goverent O	govment O
53.	gardian O	guardian O	garduan O	guarduan O
54.	anouncement O	anouncment O	announcment O	announcement O
55.	endorsment O	endorsemant O	endorsmant O	endorsement O
56.	argument O	argewment O	argumeant O	arguement O
57.	Identifycation O	Identiffication O	identification O	iddentitcation O
58.	innocent O	inocent O	innosent O	innoscent O
59.	dissapoint O	disapoint O	dissapoint O	disappoint O
60.	profesion O	proffesion O	proffession O	profession O

22

Exam Type Questions

TEST 1 (Verbal Usage) checks both spelling and grammar. It uses a series of short sentences with two blank spaces to fill in. You choose the correct pair of answers from the choices given. As with all the questions in the PIR test, speed is essential. If the question involves grammar or homophones (similar sounding words) you will need to glance through the sentence before making your choice. If the question involves simple spelling there is no need to read the sentence. For this reason, we suggest that you look at the answers before you read the sentence. Find one word that you are sure is correct, as a first step, then progress from there.

ITQ 16

Fill in the circle that goes with the correct answer. For speed, look at the choice of answers before reading the sentence. You have 5 minutes for 15 questions.

1. After taking the_____ he experienced _____.

(A)	(B)	(C)	(D)	(E)
narcotic	narcotic	narkotic	narkotic	none of these
hallusinations	hallucinations	halucinations	halusinations	

2. The climber was poorly _____ and lacked _____.

(A)	(B)	(C)	(D)	(E)
equipped	equipped	equiped	equiped	none of these
experience	experience	experience	experiance	

3. He would not _____ that he _____ driving whilst over the limit.

(A)	(B)	(C)	(D)	(E)
except	accept	accept	except	none of these
was	were	was	were	

4. Careful _____ is required for a_____ outcome.

(A)	(B)	(C)	(D)	(E)
preperation	preperation	preparation	preparation	none of these
success	sucsess	sucsess	success	

5. All three statement were _____ in their _____.

(A)	(B)	(C)	(D)	(E)
disimilar	dissimilar	dissimiler	disimiller	none of these
evidance	evidence	evidence	evidence	

6. His _____ behaviour resulted in a court _____.

(A)	(B)	(C)	(D)	(E)
willfull	willful	wilful	wilfull	none of these
appearance	appearance	appearence	appearence	

7. The man had tried to _____ the _____ goods.

(A)
disguise
counterfeit

(B)
disguise
counterfit

(C)
dissguise
counterfeit

(D)
dissgise
counterfit

(E)
none of these

8. Two_____ offences were _____.

(A)
seperate
acknowledged

(B)
separate
acknowledged

(C)
separate
acknowleged

(D)
seperate
acknowleged

(E)
none of these

9. Close_____ with the residents _____ would be essential.

(A)
co-operation
comittee

(B)
cooperation
commitee

(C)
co-operation
committee

(D)
cooperation
comitee

(E)
none of these

10. The _____ should have left it to the _____.

(A)
amateur
profesionals

(B)
amateur
professionals

(C)
amatuer
professionals

(D)
amatuer
proffessionals

(E)
none of these

11. A _____ outcome to the case was by no means _____.

(A)
successful
guaranteed

(B)
successfull
guaranteed

(C)
successful
gaurateed

(D)
succesful
gauranteed

(E)
none of these

12. Lack of _____ in car control can be _____.

(A)
proficiency
disasterous

(B)
proficiency
disastrous

(C)
profficiency
disastrous

(D)
profficieny
disasterous

(E)
none of these

13. The fireman was both _____ and _____ at the same time.

(A)
curteous
courageous

(B)
curteous
corageous

(C)
courteous
courageous

(D)
courteous
courageous

(E)
none of these

14. The_____ couple were becoming an _____.

(A)
quarelling
embarrassment

(B)
quarreling
embarassment

(C)
quarrelling
embarrassment

(D)
quarrelling
embarrasment

(E)
none of these

15. The thief's _____ was very_____ .

(A)
accompliss
conspicuous

(B)
accomplis
conspicous

(C)
acomplice
conspicious

(D)
accomplice
conspicuous

(E)
none of these

24

TEST 2 -
CHECKING INFORMATION

THE second test in the test battery involves *proof reading* i.e. checking information to see whether or not it contains mistakes. The information takes the form of names, dates and descriptions of stolen goods and includes mispelled names, incorrect dates and other errors.

In the test you will have to check if the information in one list has been accurately transferred to a second list. This is not difficult to do, but you have only a few seconds to answer each question.

For speed an accuracy we recommend that you:

i) read carefully and remember as much information as possible in one go. Do not scan back and forth between both lists, in the hope of finding a mistake, as this wastes time.

ii) move straight on to the next question if you get stuck or confused for any reason

iii) be careful to fill in the answer(s) corresponding to the question you are on.

iv) memorise the numerical equivalent of the month when converting it from a number to a word e.g. $7.8 = 7^{th}$ August.

You should be able to recognise the month that corresponding with the number and vice versa without hesitation.

January = 1	1 = January
February = 2	2 = February
March = 3	3 = March
April = 4	4 = April
May = 5	5 = May
June = 6	6 = June
July = 7	7 = July
August = 8	8 = August
September = 9	9 = September
October = 10	10 = October
November = 11	11 = November
December = 12	12 = December

ITQ 17

Fill in the circle under the name of the month that corresponds with the digit given. You have 30 seconds to answer 10 questions.

e.g.	**12**	Sept ○	Oct ○	Nov ○	Dec ●
1.	**6**	June ○	July ○	Aug ○	Sep ○
2.	**3**	Apr ○	March ○	May ○	Aug ○
3.	**10**	Sep ○	Oct ○	Nov ○	Dec ○
4.	**8**	Aug ○	Sept ○	Oct ○	Nov ○
5.	**2**	Apr ○	Jan ○	Feb ○	May ○
6.	**9**	Oct ○	Sept ○	July ○	Aug ○
7.	**7**	May ○	June ○	July ○	Aug ○
8.	**4**	May ○	Sep ○	Feb ○	Apr ○
9.	**11**	Oct ○	Nov ○	Dec ○	Jan ○
10.	**5**	June ○	July ○	May ○	Apr ○

25

ITQ 18

Fill in the circle in list 2 **if** the date has been transferred incorrectly from list 1. You have one minute to answer 20 questions

	List 1	List 2
e.g.	7.11 (Nov 7th)	Nov 9th ●
1.	8.12	Dec 12 ○
2.	21.10	Nov 12 ○
3.	20.9	Aug 20 ○
4.	4.6	Apr 6 ○
5.	5.3	March 5 ○
6.	12.10	Oct 10 ○
7.	9.10	Sept 10 ○
8.	10.9	Sept 10 ○
9.	6.6	July 6 ○
10.	7.7	July 7 ○
11.	3.8	Aug 8 ○
12.	8.3	Aug 8 ○
13.	10.12	Dec 10 ○
14.	16.9	Sept 19 ○
15.	3.5	Apr 3 ○
16.	6.5	June 5 ○
17.	10.1	Nov 1 ○
18.	20.8	Aug 20 ○
19.	23.10	Nov 23 ○
20.	6.6	June 9 ○

Memorising Numbers

Memory can be improved by a process known as *chunking*. This involves separating bits of information into more meaningful units. So for example, a seven digit telephone number such as 061693325 is much easier to memorise as three shorter sequences of digits:- 061 693 325 - particularly when the first chunk is recognised as the code for Manchester.

In Test 2 you will have to remember large numbers when checking for discrepancies. You can do this by splitting the number into two or three chunks as shown below.

Examples:-
459273 becomes 459 (four five nine), 273 (two seven three)

692008 becomes six nine two, double zero eight

123765 becomes one two three, seven six five

111249 becomes treble one, two four nine

2309785 becomes two three zero, nine seven eight five

26

ITQ 19

Compare list one with list two to check for mistakes. Fill in the circle in list two if the number has been transferred incorrectly Use a 'chunking technique' to break the number into easily remembered chunks. You have 1 minute to answer 12 questions.

List 1

1.	9473
2.	6824
3.	8492
4.	15362
5.	86555
6.	45292
7.	615755
8.	235908
9.	109827
10.	232324
11.	4675013
12.	9335485

List 2

1.	9437	O
2.	6824	O
3.	8462	O
4.	15392	O
5.	86556	O
6.	45292	O
7.	715655	O
8.	235908	O
9.	109728	O
10.	233224	O
11.	4675310	O
12.	9335485	O

ITQ 20

Compare list one with list two to check for mistakes. Fill in the circle in list two if the stolen item serial number has been transferred incorrectly. Use a 'chunking technique' to aid memory (examples in brackets). You have 1 minute to answer 12 questions.

Stolen Item Serial Numbers: List 1

1.	94JB73 (94J, B73)
2.	CW68232 (CW6, 8234)
3.	38462Y
4.	5BV1562
5.	8655TS
6.	459ZG25
7.	16575X
8.	259811LT
9.	111H987
10.	452334S
11.	QW503
12.	93354FL

Stolen Item Serial Numbers: List 2

1.	94JP73	O
2.	CW68323	O
3.	38462Y	O
4.	5BP1562	O
5.	8656TS	O
6.	459ZG25	O
7.	16565X	O
8.	259811LT	O
9.	111H978	O
10	452324S	O
11	QW530	O
12	93354FL	O

ITO 21

The table below contains information about stolen cars. This information has been transferred onto the computer and contains typing errors. Fill in the circles at the bottom of the page corresponding with the errors. Hint: check the owner and car first, and the date and engine number second (for example, Mr Whittaker Blue Austin Maestro,- *check* / 9th September engine number 1156211T - *check*). Take your time. Question 1 has been done for you.

TABLE

| 1. | Owner: Whittaker | **Mr** Mrs Miss Ms | Date: 9 September |
| | Car description: | Blue Austin Maestro | Engine no: 1156211T |

| 2. | Owner: Bushell | Mr Mrs **Miss** Ms | Date: 6 July |
| | Car description: | Red Ford Fiesta | Engine no: CH6756Q |

| 3. | Owner: Rainth | **Mr** Mrs Miss Ms | Date: 2 January |
| | Car description: | White Astra GTE | Engine no: DS3444612 |

| 4. | Owner: Corbett | Mr **Mrs** Miss Ms | Date: 24 May |
| | Car description: | Suzuki Vitara 2.0 | Engine no: AV79860 |

| 5. | Owner: Raslind | Mr Mrs Miss **Mr** | Date: 3 February |
| | Car description: | Volvo 240 Estate | Engine no: 54335697 |

COMPUTER

	Date	Description	Engine no.	Owner
1.	9/10	Brown Austin Maestro	1156211T	Mrs Whittaker
2.	6/6	Red Ford Fiesta S	CH6765Q	Ms Bushell
3.	2/1	White Astra GTe	DS344612	Mr Rainth
4.	24/5	Suzuki Vitari 2.0	AV79860	Mrs Corbett
5.	2/3	Volvo 340 Estate	54336597	Ms Raslin

	Date	Description	Engine no.	Owner	No Errors Found
1.	●	●	○	●	○
2.	○	○	○	○	○
3.	○	○	○	○	○
4.	○	○	○	○	○
5.	○	○	○	○	○

The table below contains information about stolen goods. This information has been transferred on to the computer and contains typing errors. Fill in the circles at the bottom of the page corresponding with the errors. You have only two minutes to answer six questions.

TABLE

1.	Owner: Hussain Item description:	Mr Mrs **Miss** Ms Philips Colour TV	Date: 1 November Serial no: 0874573
2.	Owner: Wilson Item description:	**Mr** Mrs Miss Ms Saracen Mountain Bike	Date: 4 March Serial no: 5673843
3.	Owner: Ferguson Item description:	**Mr** Mrs Miss Ms Black and Decker Mower	Date: 12 June Serial no: 12156324
4.	Owner: Whittle Item description:	Mr Mrs Miss **Ms** Aiwai Video Player	Date: 20 October Serial no: 6488779
5.	Owner: Walsh Item description:	**Mr** Mrs Miss Ms Praktica Camera	Date: 13 December Serial no: 3687657
6.	Owner: Davies Item description:	Mr **Mrs** Miss Ms Kenwood Hi-Fi	Date: 29 July Serial no: 9653268

COMPUTER

	Date	Description	Serial no.	Owner
1	11/1	Phillips Colour TV	8874573	Hussain Ms
2.	4/3	Sarasen Mountain Bike	5673843	Wilson Mr
3.	6/12	Black & Decker Mower	12156324	Fergusson Mr
4.	20/10	Aiwa Video Player	6488779	Whittle Mr
5.	13/12	Practika Camera	3687567	Walsh Mr
6.	19/7	Kenwood HiFi	9653268	Davis Mrs

	Date	Description	Engine no.	Owner	No Errors Found
1.	O	O	O	O	O
2.	O	O	O	O	O
3.	O	O	O	O	O
4.	O	O	O	O	O
5.	O	O	O	O	O
6.	O	O	O	O	O

This page has been deliberately left blank

TEST 4 - VERBAL REASONING

Basic Comprehension

THIS section will deal with what was formerly called a comprehension exercise and now sometimes comes under the terminology of 'understanding' or 'verbal reasoning'. Comprehension tests require *response to text*, i.e. after reading a passage of text you *elicit* facts from it and then answer questions.

The material used for test questions can be quite varied and the candidate is advised to read widely and to try to evaluate, particularly when reading a newspaper, what has actually been said. Another hint for preparation for this section is to try to *improve your reading speed* without detracting from the understanding. *The faster you can read the more time you have for answers*.

When answering comprehension type questions you should read the text carefully first, then read the question thoroughly to be certain of what is being asked, before *scanning* back through the text to try and find words or phrases which relate with those of the question. You can then extract the necessary information.

Multiple-choice type questions come with a selection of answers, and quite often, more than one answer will look plausible, however, only one answer is correct. If you know what the answer is, after reading the question, you will be able to make your choice straight away, if not, you should read through all of the answers and try to eliminate all but one of them. This is done by establishing that they are either untrue, imprecise, i.e. missing key facts, or that they are true but don't answer the question, or that they misinterpret or distort the facts. When doing this, *you may need to return to the text several times*, before choosing an answer.

ITQ 23

The following exercise will check your comprehension and reading speed. There are 5 short paragraphs each with a multiple choice type question. You should aim to answer each question in about 1 minute;

Directions: Read the passages carefully; then answer the questions that follow. Choose the answer which comes closest to saying what the passage implies. Indicate your choice by filling in the CIRCLE. See how far you can get in 5 minutes.

31

Passage 1

FOR reasons of safety, it is of prime importance that at all times drivers remain alert. For every 3 hours on the road, drivers should rest for a period of 20 minutes, sharing the driving with others if at all possible. Driving should be avoided at a time which would normally be spent resting or sleeping. It is better not to drive after a large meal, heavy exercise, and of course, after drinking alcohol. The temperature inside the vehicle should not be so high as to cause drowsiness. Sensible drivers will plan their journey in advance to minimise hold-ups which lengthen the time on the road an increase the likelihood of tiredness and frustration.

1. Drivers should avoid driving:

A. every three hours and twenty minutes. O

B. when the temperature in the car is high. O

C. at night time or when there are hold-ups. O

D. at a time normally spent sleeping. O

Do you need help?.

Answer 1 is a distortion of the facts - drivers should take a break of 20 minutes every 3 hours.

Answer 2 is imprecise/incomplete the temperature must be high enough to cause drowsiness.

Answer 3 - at night time - this is untrue - you can drive at night but should not at a time normally spent asleep. When there are hold-ups - this is misrepresentation of the facts - journeys should be planned to avoid hold-ups) i.e. only Answer 4 is true.

PROTEIN is the nutrient most concerned with the growth and repair of the body. It is a vital component of a balanced diet. About two-thirds of the protein in a UK diet comes from animal sources and one-third from vegetable sources. Animal protein has a high biological value and provides all the necessary amino acids. Vegetable protein has a low biological value and will not provide sufficient amino acids unless a variety of vegetables are eaten together. Lacto-vegetarians will take milk, cheese and eggs, so they are unlikely to suffer from inadequacy of protein. Vegans - those who do not take any food with animal connections - can have nutritional problems and must pay special attention to their diet.

2. Vegetable protein:

A. will not provide sufficient amino acids. O

B. does not have a high biological value. O

C. is not found in a UK diet. O

D. is not used for growth and repair of cells. O

HEATHROW is one of the world's busiest airports and lies sixteen miles west of London. The airport is situated on the Piccadilly Underground line at Heathrow Central station. It is also serviced by local bus and long-distance coach services. A free coach takes passengers to and from passenger terminals, where multi-storey car parks are situated for short or long-term parking. Charges for long-term parking are designed to encourage a stay of at least four hours. Commercial garages offer alternative long-term parking facilities, within easy reach of the airport.

3. Long-term parking is:

A. available at multi-storey car parks. O

B. available at or near to the airport. O

C. cheap for periods of up to four hours. O

D. free for coaches. O

Passage 4

THE railways were Britain's gift to the world. They originated from experiments in the best method of transporting coal in vast quantities from the pit-head, for iron smelting, manufacture and domestic use. In the 1820's there had been much controversy as to the rival merits of drawing coal along wooden rails by horses, or by stationary engines, or by George Stephenson's 'locomotive'. The triumph of the latter opened up opportunities not only for the carriage of all classes of goods, but also for a new method of passenger transport. Stage-coaches and canals were doomed. Short local lines laid down in the coal districts, were developed into a national system for the whole country.

4. George Stephenson's locomotive triumphed because:

A. iron rails were better than wooden ones. O

B. stagecoaches and canals were doomed. O

C. local lines were developed into a national system. O

D. vast quantities of coal could be transported. O

Passage 5

IN the eighteenth century, there were great improvements in surgery, midwifery and hygiene. At a time of benevolence, lying-in hospitals were founded in the principal towns. Country hospitals for all sorts of patients were set up. In the capital, between 1720 and 1745, Guy's, Westminster, St. George's, London and Middlesex Hospitals were all founded; the medieval St. Thomas's had been rebuilt in the reign of Queen Anne and at Bart's, teaching and the practise were improving apace. In the course of 125 years after 1700, no less than 154 new hospitals and dispensaries were established in Britain. These were not municipal under-takings; they were the outcome of the individual initiative and co-ordinated voluntary effort and subscription.

5. Hospitals were founded in the eighteenth century mainly through:

A. improvements in surgery, midwifery and hygiene. O

B. the teaching and practise of medicine. O

C. benevolent efforts. O

D. municipal undertakings. O

Exam Type Questions

IN the actual test the information you have to read will be contained within a short introductory paragraph followed by a list of facts. All you have to do is interpret the facts as presented, without making assumptions. An example is given below.

The police arrested two people at Manchester airport, suspected of drug trafficking. The people were on a flight from Thailand. The facts at this stage are:

- Class I drugs were found in their luggage.

- The two people were already known to the police and had previous convictions.

- They had a connecting flight to Holland.

- Both people were found with a large amount of cash on them.

Based on the above information, answer the following statements:-

A = TRUE	B = FALSE	C = IMPOSSIBLE TO SAY

1. The two people had previous convictions.

   ● Ⓑ Ⓒ

2. They were about to fly back to Thailand

   Ⓐ ● Ⓒ

3. The drugs had been planted on them.

   Ⓐ Ⓑ ●

Note how you have to look back at the facts three times to find the answers to three questions.

ITQ 24

Trouble broke out at the local football match. A number of people were injured. The facts at this stage are:-

- The match was a sell-out

- Rival fans were all around the ground.

- Most injuries were minor and only one person was taken to hospital.

- Surveillance cameras recorded the violent scenes.

- The ringleaders were arrested.

- A number of fans had forged tickets.

A = TRUE   B = FALSE   C = IMPOSSIBLE TO SAY

---

1. The ground had a capacity crowd.   Ⓐ Ⓑ Ⓒ
2. The fans were segregated.   Ⓐ Ⓑ Ⓒ
3. The ringleaders were caught on camera.   Ⓐ Ⓑ Ⓒ
4. There were no forged tickets.   Ⓐ Ⓑ Ⓒ
5. A person was taken to hospital.   Ⓐ Ⓑ Ⓒ
6. A policeman was injured.   Ⓐ Ⓑ Ⓒ
7. A policeman could have been injured.   Ⓐ Ⓑ Ⓒ

ITQ 25

The police were called to a road traffic accident. The only facts known at this stage are:

- Two vehicles were involved.

- Two people were injured, but not seriously.

- Both of the drivers were breathalysed.

- One of the vehicles had a defective tyre and no MOT.

A = TRUE	B = FALSE	C = IMPOSSIBLE TO SAY

1. Three cars were involved in the accident.   Ⓐ Ⓑ Ⓒ

2. Both drivers were injured.   Ⓐ Ⓑ Ⓒ

3. The injuries were not serious.   Ⓐ Ⓑ Ⓒ

4. The injured people were taken to hospital   Ⓐ Ⓑ Ⓒ

5. The car with the defective tyre caused the accident.   Ⓐ Ⓑ Ⓒ

6. The car with the defective tyre could have caused the accident.   Ⓐ Ⓑ Ⓒ

7. The car with the defective tyre definitely caused the accident   Ⓐ Ⓑ Ⓒ

Police were called to the scene of a burglary at a large computer factory. The facts known so far are:-

- £20,000 of computers were stolen.

- The burglar alarms did not go off.

- A large white van was seen driving away from the factory at speed, in the early hours.

- The company was very well insured.

- One of the employees has a criminal record. His name is Kevin Smith.

- A plan of the factory and wiring diagrams were found in one of the staff's lockers, a man called John Barker.

- Kevin Smith and John Barker are friends.

- A PNC check revealed that Kevin Smith owns a white van.

A = TRUE	B = FALSE	C = IMPOSSIBLE TO SAY

1. Kevin Smith and John Barker are employees of the company. (A) (B) (C)

2. The computers were not insured. (A) (B) (C)

3. The large white van could be Kevin Smith's (A) (B) (C)

4. John Barker has an alibi. (A) (B) (C)

5. Kevin Smith and John Barker are prime suspects. (A) (B) (C)

6. Kevin Smith is definitely to blame. (A) (B) (C)

ANSWERS TO ITQ's

ITQ 1
1. hit
2. drive
3. drink
4. open
5. are
6. am
7. is
8. is

ITQ 2
1. speak, speak, speaks
2. laugh, laugh
3. write, write, write

ITQ 3
1. boy
2. shops
3. Prime Minister, Monday
4. Prime Minister, Tony Blair
5. Morning, newspaper
6. meal, chopsticks, spoon
7. Bob, English, French, German

ITQ 4
1. D
2. C
3. D
4. A
5. D
6. C
7. A

ITQ 5
1. She wrote it.
2. He closed it.
3. He met her.
4. She made it for him.
5. They posted them.
6. They came to see us.

ITQ 6
1. I   her
2. I
3. me
4. they   us
5. I
6. me   we   them

ITQ 7
1. he
2. she
3. they
4. I   he

ITQ 8
1. braver
2. harder
3. easier
4. larger
5. worst
6. more
7. better
8. best

ITQ 9
1. Tom's
2. Farmer's
3. neighbour's
4. animals'
5. yachts'
6. men's
7. fishermen's

ITQ 10
1. he's
2. that's
3. I'm
4. they're
5. we'll
6. they'll
7. there's
8. we've
9. who's

ITQ 11

1. does not
2. were not
3. have not
4. we are
5. when is
6. I would
7. cannot
8. it is
9. we will
10. I will

ITQ 12

1. "Come inside this minute," shouted the boy's mother.

2. "That's very kind of you," he said cheerfully.

3. My brother said, "I can't make it."

4. "Good morning," said Mr Evans. "I am pleased with your progress. You must have a pay rise."

5. "I must go," said Mary "because I am meeting my husband shortly."

6. "I hit the ball over the boundary," said Boycott "and no one can find it."

7. "Hey you boy!" he yelled. "Come here. I'm fed up with your misbehaviour."

ITQ 13

1. risen   begun
2. thrown   stolen
3. written   eaten
4. drank   went
5. sank   run
6. driven
7. frozen

ITQ14

1. there
2. plain
3. whole
4. waste
5. through
6. practice
7. licence
8. scene

ITQ 15

1. B
2. B
3. B
4. C
5. C
6. B
7. B
8. C
9. C
10. D
11. C
12. C
13. C
14. B
15. B
16. B
17. B
18. D
19. D
20. D
21. C
22. C
23. C
24. C
25. C

44

26. C
27. C
28. A
29. A
30. B
31. B
32. B
33. B
34. B
35. B
36. B
37. A
38. A
39. A
40. A
41. D
42. C
43. A
44. A
45. A
46. C
47. D
48. B
49. B
50. B
51. A
52. B
53. B
54. D
55. D
56. A
57. C
58. A
59. D
60. D

ITQ16
1. B
2. C
3. C
4. D
5. B
6. E
7. A

8. B
9. C
10. B
11. A
12. B
13. C
14. C
15. D

ITQ 17
1. June
2. March
3. October
4. August
5. February
6. September
7. July
8. April
9. November
10. May

ITQ 18
1. ●
2. ●
3. ●
4. ●
5. O
6. ●
7. ●
8. O
9. ●
10. O
11. ●
12. ●
13. O
14. ●
15. ●
16. ●
17. ●
18. O
19. ●
20. ●

ITQ 19
1. ●
2. ○
3. ●
4. ●
5. ●
6. ○
7. ●
8. ○
9. ●
10. ●
11. ●
12. ○

ITQ 20
1. ●
2. ●
3. ○
4. ●
5. ●
6. ○
7. ●
8. ○
9. ●
10. ●
11. ●
12. ○

ITQ 21
1. ● ● ○ ● ○
2. ● ● ● ● ○
3. ○ ● ● ○ ○
4. ○ ● ○ ○ ○
5. ● ● ● ● ○

ITQ 22
1. ● ● ● ● ○
2. ○ ● ○ ○ ○
3. ● ● ○ ● ○
4. ○ ● ○ ● ○
5. ○ ● ● ○ ○
6. ● ● ○ ● ○

ITQ 23
1. D
2. B
3. B
4. D
5. C

ITQ 24
1. A
2. B
3. A
4. B
5. A
6. C
7. A

ITQ 25
1. B
2. C
3. A
4. C
5. C
6. A
7. B

ITQ 26
1. A
2. B
3. A
4. C
5. B
6. B

Part 2

OBSERVATIONAL SKILLS

(For the Police Initial Recruitment Test -PIRT)

First Published 1998
Second Edition
Copyright © 2001 ELC Publications

TEST 5 - OBSERVATION TESTS

IN Test 5 of the PIR test battery, you will have to watch a short video of life-like scenes, then answer a series of questions which check your observation skills and ability to recall details.

Memory and recollection vary from person to person. Take three average citizens, with a similar degree of honesty and integrity and ask them to make a statement concerning a bank raid which they have all witnessed. Whilst the three statements will contain a fair degree of concurrence there will also be areas of dissimilarity. The reason for the dissimilarity will often revolve around what they thought they saw rather than what actually happened.

An important factor, therefore, in order to improve your observation skills is to train yourself to *observe accurately* by watching an event, however trivial, and then jotting down immediately what you saw. A neighbour hanging washing on a line, or the postman's progress down the road would make suitable models. The information you record should be clear and precise. Try filing details in the form of *who, what, where, when, how and why.* Personalise your notes so that they mean particular things to you. You should be able to reconstruct partial images from your notes at a later date.

Clear and precise information is also required when giving instructions. How often, in an unfamiliar district, has the reader stopped a passing stranger for simple and clear directions? How often also have the replies been unclear, rambling accompanied by wild gesticulations. The underlying principle behind all language is communication and it does not matter how clear the route is in the eye of the director, if the recipient fails to understand, the communication has failed.

When a person observes an event, not only are their cognitive (or thinking) powers involved but also their emotions are involved, this applies particularly when an incident observed is of an unpleasant nature. It is important not to confuse facts with opinions and to clearly preface opinions with *I believe, I think* or similar words.

Emotional stress can impair memory. In our primitive ancestors stress had a survival value. It prepared us physically to face or flee a danger ('flight or fight' syndrome). Today's 'stressors' are more likely to be perceived threats to an individual's well-being and self-esteem rather than actual threats to survival. However, any stressful situation, real or apparent, triggers many of the same effects, for example, increased blood pressure/heart rate, and anxiety.

The level of stress you experience depends upon your ability to cope with the situation. Response to stress is influenced by personality (way of thinking, behaving, et cetera) and social environment. What one person finds stressful, another may find

1

stimulating. Managing your own stress depends in part upon becoming aware of what your own particular stressors are. You can then confront each situation and try to change it and/or change your thoughts and emotional reactions to the stressor, so as to lessen its impact. Emotional support from family, friends and work colleagues leads to an improvement in coping with stress.

Stress felt in the examination room can lead to a loss of concentration and reduced short-term memory. This probably results from 'retrieval failure'. - The information is in your memory, but you cannot get at it. The stress of the situation has impaired your ability to retrieve information and it is 'forgotten'.

Try to remain calm and relaxed in the examination room. Observe details and file them away under who, what, where, when, how and why. Where possible, use personal memories from real incidents in your past as 'memory hooks'. Short-term memory improves if you repeat the information to yourself several times. Be aware that it is much easier to remember what you have seen than what you have heard.

Don't worry if feel that your memory is not up to scratch! Multiple choice type questions are not too difficult to answer. Memories can be triggered from several sources and the choice of answers acts as a memory *cue*. Multiple choice tests do not require full recollection. You need only to *match* the information encountered against one of the answers given.

This course does not include a video, instead we have included a series of *stills*. These depict various scenes in line drawings, both black and white and with spot colour. The memory and observation skills tested for are similar to those that you will require in PIR test.

Instructions for the ITQ's
The first ITQ in this section shows a black and white picture of an accident scene. This scene was witnessed by you as you stepped off a bus. Study the picture for <u>30 seconds only</u>. Try to memorise everything that you see, paying attention to the <u>details</u>. The police will ask you for a statement about what you saw.

After 30 seconds, turn over the page until you reach the multiple choice questions. Do not turn back to the picture. When you have answered the questions, turn over the page to check and mark your answers. Repeat this process for the remaining ITQ's.

You have 4 minutes to answer three ITQ's (includes time for marking).

Read through the instructions once <u>more</u>, then turn over the next page.

This page has been deliberately left blank.

This page has been deliberately left blank.

ITQ 1

Look at the picture for 30 seconds, then turn over the page.

This page has been deliberately left blank.

This page has been deliberately left blank.

This page has been deliberately left blank.

Now answer the following questions
(fill in the correct circle)

1. When the accident took place, you:

   (A) were just getting on the bus.
   (B) were just getting off the bus.
   (C) had got off the bus.

2. When the accident took place, two children:

   (A) had just crossed the road.
   (B) were just about to cross the road.
   (C) were just crossing the road.

3. When the accident took place, a cyclist:

   (A) had just overtaken the bus.
   (B) was just overtaking the bus.
   (C) was just going to overtake the bus.

4. When the accident took place, an elderly lady:

   (A) had just crossed the road.
   (B) was just crossing the road.
   (C) was just about to cross the road.

5. When the accident took place, a woman with a dog:

   (A) had just about crossed the road.
   (B) was just about to cross the road.
   (C) was just crossing the road.

6. When the accident took place, a man:

   (A) was just getting out of a car.
   (B) was just getting in a car.
   (C) had just got out of a car.

7. When the accident took place, a milk float:

   (A) was just turning left.
   (B) had just turned left.
   (C) was just going to turn left.

9

This page has been deliberately left blank.

ANSWERS TO ITQ 1

1. **B** - you were just getting off the bus
2. **A** - had just crossed the road
3. **B** - was just overtaking the bus
4. **B** - was just crossing the road
5. **A** - had just about crossed the road
6. **A** - was just getting out of car.
7. **C** - was just going to turn left.

This page has been deliberately left blank.

This page has been deliberately left blank.

This page has been deliberately left blank.

Now answer the following questions
(fill in the correct circle)

1. The cyclist was wearing:

    (A) a yellow helmet
    (B) a red helmet
    (C) a blue helmet

2. The car at the crossing was:

    (A) a green hatchback
    (B) a brown hatchback
    (C) a grey hatchback

3. The woman with a dog had:

    (A) brown hair
    (B) black hair
    (C) blonde hair

4. The milk float was painted:

    (A) blue
    (B) green
    (C) red

5. The man climbing out of his car had:

    (A) red hair
    (B) blond hair
    (C) brown hair

6. The elderly lady at the crossing:

    (A) dropped a brown handbag
    (B) dropped a black handbag
    (C) dropped a brown umbrella

This page has been deliberately left blank.

ANSWERS TO ITQ 2

1. **B** - a red helmet
2. **A** - a green hatchback
3. **C** - blonde hair
4. **A** - blue
5. **C** - brown hair
6. **B** - dropped a black handbag

This page has been deliberately left blank.

Look at the picture for 1 minute, then turn over the page.
<u>Concentrate on any numbers you can see.</u>

21

This page has been deliberately left blank.

This page has been deliberately left blank.

This page has been deliberately left blank.

Now answer the following questions
(fill in the correct circle)

1. The time on the clock was:

   (A) 11.30
   (B) 12.30
   (C) 13.30

2. The date on the calendar was:

   (A) August 8th
   (B) August 18th
   (C) August 28th

3. According to a newspaper, the number of people killed was:

   (A) 30
   (B) 130
   (C) 230

4. A double room costs:

   (A) £40
   (B) £50
   (C) £60

5. The earliest time for breakfast was:

   (A) 6.30
   (B) 7.00
   (C) 7.30

6. The woman entering the lift was holding key number:

   (A) 21
   (B) 31
   (C) 41

7. The Jeep registration plate read:

   (A) THX 1318
   (B) XTH 1183
   (C) THX 1138

This page has been deliberately left blank.

ANSWERS TO ITQ 3

1. **A** - the time on the clock was 11.30
2. **A** - the date was August 8th
3. **B** - the number of people killed was 130
4. **C** - a double room costs £60
5. **C** - the earliest time for breakfast was 7.30
6. **B** - the woman was holding key number 31
7. **C** - the Jeep registration plate read THX 1138

Part 3

<u>BASIC NUMERICAL SKILLS</u>

(For the Police Initial Recruitment Test -PIRT)

First Published 1998
Second Edition
Copyright © 2001 ELC Publications

Contents

Numeracy

INTRODUCTION

THIS section teaches the numerical skills which are commonly tested for. Mature candidates may have had little experience of numerical work since leaving school, so this section starts at a very simple level. However, it is not intended to be a remedial course for people with numeracy problems.

The maths skills necessary for the test do not exceed GCSE or 'O'-level standard. You need only the four basic skills of arithmetic, namely addition, subtraction, multiplication and division when solving problems. These skills can be applied to whole numbers, fractions and decimal numbers.

You are NOT allowed to use a calculator in the test, so it is vital that you understand basic arithmetic processes and can work quickly and competently with numbers, i.e. solve problems 'in your head' using *mental arithmetic*.

After completing this section, you will be familiar with the key topics of arithmetic, fractions, decimals, percentages, the metric system, graphs and charts, patterns and series. Knowledge of these topics will ensure that you have the confidence and ability in all aspects of numeracy required for the test. Importantly, you should be able to work quickly, answering the test questions without hesitation.

NUMBERS AND PLACE VALUE

STARTING at the simplest level, our number system is easily understood if you consider 'place value' where each number O to 9 is written in a column - units, tens, hundreds, thousands etc.

Examples:

Thou. Hun. Tens. Units.

| | 1 | 0 | 7 |

(one hundred and seven)

| 7 | 2 | 0 | 0 |

(seven thousand two hundred)

| | | 2 | 5 |

(twenty five)

ITQ 1

Write out the numbers in figures.

1. one thousand one hundred and sixty eight

Ans_____

2. nine thousand and forty two

Ans_____

3. one thousand and nine

Ans_____

- The answers are found at the end of this section. If you have got any answers wrong you may have a numeracy problem and require remedial help.

1

WORKING WITH NUMBERS

Addition

Numbers to be added must be arranged underneath each other so that the unit columns are in line.

Example: 139 + 226

the first step is to align the numbers in columns:

$$1 \mid 3 \mid 9$$
$$2 \mid 2 \mid 6 +$$

then we add the units column (right-hand column) $6 + 9 = 15$. The five is placed in the units column and the one ten carried over as one 'ten' into the tens column.

$$\begin{array}{r} 1\ 3\ 9 \\ 2\ 2\ 6+ \\ \hline 5 \\ \hline 1 \end{array}$$

Now we add the tens column (middle column) remembering to include the 'one' that has been carried:
$1 + 2 + 3 = 6$ (middle column) giving:

$$\begin{array}{r} 1\ 3\ 9 \\ 2\ 2\ 6+ \\ \hline 6\ 5 \\ \hline 1 \end{array}$$

Now we add the hundreds column
$2 + 1 = 3$ to give (left-hand column)

$$\begin{array}{r} 1\ 3\ 9 \\ 2\ 2\ 6+ \\ \hline 1\ 6\ 5 \\ \hline 1 \end{array}$$

For the addition of three or more numbers, the method is the same.
e.g. $200 + 86 + 44$ becomes

$$\begin{array}{r} 2\ 0\ 0 \\ 8\ 6 \\ 4\ 4+ \\ \hline 3\ 3\ 0 \\ \hline 1\ \ 1 \end{array}$$

Now try the following ITQ using the method described above. You must not use a calculator; try to work out the answer 'in your head' if possible, otherwise do your working out on a separate sheet of paper or in the space available.

ITQ 2

Work out the following sums.

1. Six added to eight makes...

Ans_____

2.   22 added to 64 gives...

Ans_____

3.   100 plus 10 equals...

Ans_____

4.   409 ı 24 = ...

Ans_____

5.   250 + 17800 = ...

Ans_____

Subtraction

Subtraction is concerned with taking things away. Subtraction is the reverse of addition. The most important thing about subtraction is that the larger number is on top (above the smaller), i.e. when subtracting you SUBTRACT THE SMALLEST NUMBER FROM THE BIGGEST NUMBER.

As with addition, the numbers must be arranged underneath each other, so that the units columns are in line. After aligning the numbers, we subtract (take-away) the columns vertically starting at the right-hand end (units column). For example:

$$374 - 126$$

The first step is to align the numbers:

$$
\begin{array}{c c c}
3 & 7 & 4 \\
1 & 2 & 6 -
\end{array}
$$

then we subtract the units column (right-hand column) 4 - 6 we cannot do since six is larger than four.

To overcome this problem we borrow one from the tens column (this is the same as ten units) and add it to the four in the units column. So our sum now becomes:

$$14 - 6 \text{ (we can do)} = 8$$

so far we can write

$$
\begin{array}{c c c}
3 & 7 & _14 \\
1 & 2 & 6 - \\
\hline
 & & 8
\end{array}
$$

The next step is to pay back the 'one' we have just borrowed from the tens column. There are two methods for doing this and both are explained below.

Method 1 (old fashioned method - most popular)

In this method the ten is paid back to the bottom, for example

$$
\begin{array}{c c c}
3 & 7 & _14 \\
1 & 2_1 & 6 - \\
\hline
 & & 8
\end{array}
$$

Now we add the 1 and the 2 to make 3. The 3 is subtracted from the 7 to give to the 4. So the sum becomes:-

$$
\begin{array}{c c c}
3 & 7 & _14 \\
1 & 2_1 & 6 - \\
\hline
 & 4 & 8
\end{array}
$$

Finally we subtract the 1 from 3 (in the hundreds column) to give 2 i.e.

$$
\begin{array}{c c c}
3 & 7 & _14 \\
1 & 2_1 & 6 - \\
\hline
2 & 4 & 8
\end{array}
$$

Method 2 (modern method)

In this method the ten borrowed is subtracted as a one at the top of the tens column (7-1 = 6) i.e.

$$
\begin{array}{c c c}
3 & \overset{6}{\not{7}}_1 & 4 \\
1 & 2 & 6 - \\
\hline
2 & 4 & 8
\end{array}
$$

ITQ 3

Work out the following subtraction sums ('in your head' ifs possible) .

1. 9 take-away 7 leaves...

Ans_____

2. 65 take-away 21 leaves...

Ans_____

3. Subtracting 67 from 94 gives...

Ans_____

4. 718 minus 618 equals...

Ans_____

5. 1427 less 300 equals ...

Ans_____

6. 6742 - 5630 =

Ans_____

To work with multiplication sums you need to be familiar with your "Times Tables" - the most common times tables are shown on the next page. It is essential that you memorise these tables because calculators are not allowed in the examination room.

Below the times tables you will find a Multiplication Table which is a handy way of finding the answer (known as the 'product') when any two numbers from 0 to 12 are multiplied together. See is you can find out how to use it - it's not difficult!

Notice that 0 times any number is always 0.

Multiplication

Multiplication (or 'times') means "lots of", and is a quick way of adding up numbers which have an equal value.

For example:
5 multiplied by three 3 = 5 + 5 + 5
Note that 5 x 3 = 15 and 3 x 5 = 15

This applies to all numbers that are multiplied together, it doesn't matter which way around you put them, the answer is the same.

THE COMMON TIMES TABLES

2 times	3 times	4 times	5 times	6 times	7 times
1x2 = 2	1x3 = 3	1x4 = 4	1x5 = 5	1x6 = 6	1x7 = 7
2x2 = 4	2x3 = 6	2x4 = 8	2x5 = 10	2x6 =12	2x7 = 14
3x2 = 6	3x3 = 9	3x4 = 12	3x5 = 15	3x6 = 18	3x7 = 21
4x2 = 8	4x3 = 12	4x4 = 16	4x5 = 20	4x6 = 24	4x7 = 28
5x2 = 10	5x3 = 15	5x4 = 20	5x5 = 25	5x6 = 30	5x7 = 35
6x2 = 12	6x3 = 18	6x4 = 24	6x5 = 30	6x6 = 36	6x7 = 42
7x2 = 14	7x3 = 21	7x4 = 28	7x5 = 35	7x6 = 42	7x7 = 49
8x2 = 16	8x3 = 24	8x4 = 32	8x5 = 40	8x6 = 48	8x7 = 56
9x2 = 18	9x3 = 27	9x4 = 36	9x5 = 45	9x6 = 54	9x7 = 63
0x2 = 20	10x3 = 30	10x4 = 40	10x5 = 50	10x6 = 60	10x7 = 70
11x2 = 22	11x3 = 33	11x4 = 44	11x5 = 55	11x6 = 66	11x7 = 77
12x2 = 24	12x3 = 36	12x4 = 48	12x5 = 60	12x6 = 72	12x7 = 84

8 times	9 times	10 times	11 times	12 times
1x8 = 8	1x9 = 9	1x10 = 10	1x11 = 11	1x12 = 12
2x8 = 16	2x9 = 18	2x10 = 20	2x11 = 22	2x12 = 24
3x8 = 24	3x9 = 27	3x10 = 30	3x11 = 33	3x12 = 36
4x8 = 32	4x9 = 36	4x10 = 40	4x11 = 44	4x12 = 48
5x8 = 40	5x9 = 45	5x10 = 50	5x11 = 55	5x12 = 60
6x8 = 48	6x9 = 54	6x10 = 60	6x11 = 66	6x12 = 72
7x8 = 56	7x9 = 63	7x10 = 70	7x11 = 77	7x12 = 84
8x8 = 64	8x9 = 72	8x10 = 80	8x11 = 88	8x12 = 96
9x8 = 72	9x9 = 81	9x10 = 90	9x11 = 99	9x12 =108
10x8 = 80	10x9 = 90	10x10 = 100	10x11 = 110	10x12 = 120
11x8 = 88	11x9 = 99	11x10 = 110	11x11 = 121	11x12 = 132
12x8 = 96	12x9 = 108	12x10 = 120	12x11 = 132	12x12 = 144

MULTIPLICATION TABLE (try to memorise)

	1	2	3	4	5	6	7	8	9	10	11	12
1	1	2	3	4	5	6	7	8	9	10	11	12
2	2	4	6	8	10	12	14	16	18	21	22	24
3	3	6	9	12	15	18	21	24	27	30	33	36
4	4	8	12	16	20	24	28	32	36	40	44	48
5	5	10	15	20	25	30	35	40	45	50	55	60
6	6	12	18	24	30	36	42	48	54	60	66	72
7	7	14	21	28	35	42	49	56	63	70	77	84
8	8	16	24	32	40	48	56	64	72	80	88	96
9	9	18	27	36	45	54	63	72	81	90	99	108
10	10	20	30	40	50	60	70	80	90	100	110	120
11	11	22	33	44	55	66	77	88	99	110	121	132
12	12	24	36	48	60	72	84	96	108	120	132	144

Short Multiplication

This is multiplication of any number by a unit (any number from 1 to 9).

Examples are:

$$3 \times 8$$
$$32 \times 4$$
$$108 \times 9$$
$$524 \times 3$$

↑All units

For example: 19 x 3
we write the sum as:

$$
\begin{array}{r}
1\,9 \\
3\,\times \\
\end{array}
$$

First we multiply the 9 by the 3 to give 27

9 x 3 = 27 (see three times table)

As with addition the seven is written in the units column and the 2 is carried as 2 tens into the tens column as follows:

$$
\begin{array}{r}
1\,9 \\
\underline{3\,\times} \\
\underline{7} \\
{\scriptstyle 2}
\end{array}
$$

Now we multiply the 1 by the 3 to give 3 (1 x 3 = 3). This 3 is added to the 2 previously carried to the tens column to give 5 (3 + 2 = 5). So the finished sum becomes:

$$
\begin{array}{r}
1\,9 \\
\underline{3\,\times} \\
\underline{5\,7} \\
{\scriptstyle 2}
\end{array}
$$

i.e. 19 x 3 = 57

Progressing a stage further, what is 68 x 9?

We re-write the sum as in previous examples giving us:

$$
\begin{array}{r}
6\,8 \\
9\,\times \\
\end{array}
$$

Multiplying the units gives 8 x 9 = 72 (see nine times table) so we have:

$$
\begin{array}{r}
6\,8 \\
\underline{9\,\times} \\
\underline{2} \\
{\scriptstyle 7}
\end{array}
$$

We now multiply the 6 in the tens column by the 9 to give 6 x 9 = 54

The 54 is added to the 7 previously carried, to give 54 + 7 = 61. The 1 of the 61 is placed in the tens column and the 6 of the 61 is carried into the hundreds column:

$$
\begin{array}{r}
6\,8 \\
\underline{9\,\times} \\
\underline{1\,2} \\
{\scriptstyle 6\ 7}
\end{array}
$$

Since there are no hundreds to multiply in the hundreds column, the figure 6 can be carried directly into this column giving

$$
\begin{array}{r}
6\,8 \\
\underline{9\,\times} \\
\underline{6\,1\,2} \\
{\scriptstyle 6\ 7}
\end{array}
$$

6

Calculate the following sums:

1. Multiply 6 by 2

Ans_____

2. Multiply 23 by 4

Ans_____

3. 90 times 5 is...

Ans_____

4. The product of 19 and 5 is...

Ans_____

5. 33 x 3 = ...

Ans_____

Long Multiplication
This is multiplying any number by a number greater than 9, for example 52 x 18; 120 x 50 etc

To multiply 52 x 18 we re-write this as:

$$\begin{array}{r} 5\,2 \\ \underline{1\,8}\,\text{x} \\ \underline{} \end{array}$$

We proceed in two steps as follows: first by multiplying the 52 by the 8 in the units column and second by multiplying the 52 by the 1 in the tens column.

1st step: (multiply 52 by the 8) so we have

$$\begin{array}{r} 5\,2 \\ \underline{1\,8}\,\text{x} \\ \underline{4\,1\,6} \\ \scriptstyle 1 \end{array}$$

2nd step: (multiply the 52 by the 1 in the tens column). Since we are now multiplying from the tens column we leave the units column blank which is the same as filling it with a 0. The sum is written on the line below 416

$$\begin{array}{r} 5\,2 \\ \underline{1\,8}\,\text{x} \\ 4\,1\,6 \\ 5\,2\,0 \end{array}$$

We now add the two steps together i.e. add 416 and 520 to give the final sum which is shown below.

$$\begin{array}{r} 5\,2 \\ \underline{1\,8}\,\text{x} \\ 4\,1\,6 \\ \underline{5\,2\,0} \\ 9\,3\,6 \end{array}$$

ITQ 5

Work out the following multiplication sums.

1. 62 x 13

$$\begin{array}{r} 62 \\ 13 \times \\ \hline \end{array}$$

Ans_____

2. 79 x 32

Ans_____

3. 80 x 15

Ans_____

4. 254 x 20

Ans_____

Division

Division is the reverse of multiplication and is concerned with sharing (or dividing numbers into equal parts). For example, divide 195 by 3, i.e. 195 ÷3

We write this as follows:-

$$3\overline{)195}$$

The first step is to divide the 1 by the three. However, since 3's into 1 won't

go we have to carry the 1 into the next column, i.e.

$$3\overline{)1^19}\quad \text{giving us 3's into 19}$$

We now use the multiplication table in reverse to find how many 3's are in 19. To do this start in the 3's column on the left-hand side and move along the horizontal row until you get to the number which is closest to but smaller than 19. The number is 18. Following the vertical row upwards gives us 6. So 3 goes into 19 six times with 1 left over (19-18 =1[left over]). The 6 is placed at the top and the 1 is carried to the next column, making 15, i.e.

$$3\overline{)1^19^15}^{\,6}$$

Finally the 3 is divided into 15. The three times table shows us that 3 goes into 15 times exactly, so the finished sum is:

$$3\overline{)1^19^15}^{\,6\,5}$$

- note that the answer, in this case 65, is sometimes called the *quotient* . We can check if the answer is correct by multiplying the quotient by the number we have divided by (65x3 = 195 i.e. correct).

8

ITQ 6

Find the quotient

1. $36 \div 9$

Ans_____

2. $248 \div 4$

Ans_____

3. $3\overline{)339}$

Ans_____

4. $5\overline{)265}$

Ans_____

Long Division
(division by large numbers)
e.g. 2064 divided by 48

we write $48\overline{)2064}$

1st step: divide 2 by 48 - won't go
2nd step: divide 20 by 48 - won't go
3rd step: divide 206 by 48 - will go
48 into 206 will go, but we don't have
a times table for 48 so we have to
build up a table ourselves. This is
done as follows:

$1 \times 48 = 48$
$2 \times 48 = 96$
$3 \times 48 = 144$
$4 \times 48 = 192$ (the nearest to 206)
$5 \times 48 = 240$ (too big)

4th step: work out the remainder.
We know that 48 goes into 206 four
times (giving 192 as the quotient).
The remainder is given by 206 - 192
which equals 14. In long division this
is written as:-

$$
\begin{array}{r}
4 \\
48\overline{)2064} \\
192- \\
\hline
14
\end{array}
$$

5th step: we now bring the 4 down to
give 144:

$$
\begin{array}{r}
4 \\
48\overline{)2064} \\
192- \\
\hline
144
\end{array}
$$

6th step: the 48 is divided into 144 to
give 3 with no remainder (see 48
times table above)

$$
\begin{array}{r}
43 \\
48\overline{)2064} \\
192- \\
\hline
144 \\
144-
\end{array}
$$

i.e. $2064 \div 48 = 43$

ITQ 7

Work out the following long division sums

1. $360 \div 12$

Ans_____

2. $372 \div 12$

Ans_____

3. $18\overline{)792}$

Ans_____

4. $20\overline{)900}$

Ans_____

4. $72\overline{)1440}$

Ans_____

By now you should be familiar with the four basic rules of arithmetic i.e. how to add, subtract, multiply and divide numbers. The final section of this pack shows you how some of these mathematical skills can be used in practise.

Addition and division are used to work out averages as described below.

AVERAGES

The average of a group of numbers is a number having a value midway in the group and is given by:

the sum of all the numbers divided by the number of numbers in the group

Average = the sum of all the no's
                     the number of no's

this line means divided by

e.g. What is the average of the following numbers:- 5,3,6,2,4

sum of no's $= 5 + 3 + 6 + 2 + 4 = 20$
number of no's $= 5$
Average $= 20 \div 5$
Average $= 4$

e.g. What is the average of the following numbers:-

50,2,11,16,7,24,17,33
sum of numbers $= 50 + 2 + 11 + 16 + 7 + 24 + 17 + 33 = 160$

Or the sum of the numbers can be written as

$$\begin{array}{r} 50 \\ 2 \\ 11 \\ 16 \\ 7 \\ 24 \\ 17 \\ \underline{33} + \\ \underline{160} \end{array}$$

The number of numbers $= 8$
Average $= 160 \div 8 = 20$

ITQ 8

Work out the average of the following group of numbers.

1.   2,3,4

Ans_____

2.   9,7,2,6,1

Ans_____

3.   20,30,40

Ans_____

'BoDMAS' -
Order of Working out Problems

B = Brackets;
D = Division;
M = Multiplication;
A = Addition;
S = Subtraction

There is a definite order in which to work out a mathematical sum containing more than on arithmetic sign. **The rule is:** Brackets first followed by division or multiplication and then addition or subtraction.

e.g. **(7 + 14)** x 2 = **21** x 2 = 42
- note how the brackets are worked out first to give 21 before multiplying by the 2.

e.g. 7 + **14 x 2** = 7 + **28** = 35
- here the 14 is multiplied by the two to give 28 before the seven is added.

ITQ 9

Work out the problems below (use the 'BoDMAS' rule). Always work out the brackets first before doing the rest of the sum. Try to work out the answers 'in your head' if possible.

1.   5 x 6 – 2 = _____

2.   20 + 8 – 6 x 2 = _____

3.*   5(6 – 2) = _____

4.   10(41– 19) + 23 –16 ÷2 = _____

(*tip: when a number is placed directly outside a bracket this should be taken as meaning multiplied by, - the 'x' sign is frequently omitted in this way.)

11

FRACTIONS

WE use fractions in everyday situations, for example, we about half an hour, three quarters of mile or shops selling goods with a discount of one third.

$$\frac{1}{2}\text{hour} \qquad \frac{3}{4}\text{mile} \qquad \frac{1}{3}\text{discount}$$

You will be familiar with these everyday examples of fractions. Each of these fractions consists of part of the whole, i.e. part of an hour, part of a mile and part of the price.

So a fraction is: the whole divided into a number of equal parts.

All fractions have a top and bottom number. The top number is known as the NUMERATOR and the bottom number is known as the DENOMINATOR. The denominator tells us how many equal parts the whole is divided into. The numerator tells us how many parts we have.

So, for example, half an hour means that we divide the hour into two equal parts and we have one part.

An easy way to understand fractions is to draw the whole in diagram form and shade in the fraction. For example:-

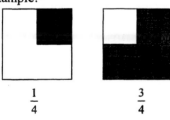

$$\frac{1}{4} \qquad\qquad \frac{3}{4}$$

Addition, Subtraction, Multiplication and Division

The four basic mathematical skills of addition, subtraction, multiplication and division, which were applied to whole numbers earlier, can also be applied to fractions.

Addition and subtraction of fractions can be dealt with together as the same "rules" apply to both. However, multiplication and division of fractions have different rules and will be explained in a separate section.

Addition and Subtraction

To be able to add or subtract fractions they must have the same bottom numbers (denominators). Taking the following example:

$$\frac{1}{8} + \frac{3}{8} \qquad \text{both fractions have a}$$

denominator of 8. We write the denominator once, and then add the two top numbers

i.e. $\dfrac{1}{8} + \dfrac{3}{8} = \dfrac{1+3}{8} = \dfrac{4}{8}$

two other examples are:-

$$\frac{3}{8} + \frac{4}{8} = \frac{3+4}{8} = \frac{7}{8}$$

$$\frac{13}{16} + \frac{5}{16} = \frac{13-5}{16} = \frac{8}{16}$$

Add the following fractions.

1. $\dfrac{6}{8} + \dfrac{1}{8}$

Ans_____

2. $\dfrac{1}{6} + \dfrac{3}{6}$

Ans_____

3. $\dfrac{7}{10} - \dfrac{3}{10}$

Ans_____

If the fractions have different denominators we can still add or subtract them, but in order to do so we first of all have to find a COMMON DENOMINATOR, i.e. a number which both denominators will divide into. Taking the following example:

$$\frac{1}{4} + \frac{3}{6}$$

then we can see that the first fraction has a denominator of 4 and the second fraction has a denominator of 6. The COMMON DENOMINATOR is a number which both 4 and 6 will divide into.

There are many numbers which both 4 and 6 will divide into. To find them we compare the four times table with six times table and see where they give us the same answer. From these tables, we can see that 4

and 6 have common denominators at 12, 24, 36 and 48. To make the working easier we choose the lowest of these i.e. 12.

4 Times Table	6 Times Table
1 x 4 = 4	1 x 6 = 6
2 x 4 = 8	2 x 6 = **12**
3 x 4 = **12**	3 x 6 = 18
4 x 4 = 16	4 x 6 = **24**
5 x 4 = 20	5 x 6 = 30
6 x 4 = **24**	6 x 6 = **36**
7 x 4 = 28	7 x 6 = 42
8 x 4 = 32	8 x 6 = **48**
9 x 4 = **36**	9 x 6 = 54
10 x 4 = 40	10 x 6 = 60
11 x 4 = 44	11 x 6 = 66
12 x 4 = **48**	12 x 6 = 72

The above tables show us that 12 is the Lowest Common Denominator (LCD). To proceed with the sum, the next stage is to re-write each fraction in terms of the common denominator, i.e. twelfths. So we re-write $\frac{1}{4}$ in twelfths and $\frac{3}{6}$ in twelfths

To do this we divide the common denominator, i.e. 12, by the denominators of the of the two fractions (i.e. 4 and 6 in the above example) and then multiply the numerator of each fraction by the respective answer.

We re-write $\frac{1}{4}$ in twelfths as follows:

$12 \div 4 = 3$ (-common denominator of 12 $\div$ denominator of 4 = 3)

$3 \times 1 = 3$ (-answer 3 x numerator of 1 = 3)

so we have:- $\dfrac{1}{4} = \dfrac{3}{12}$

Similarly: $\frac{3}{6}$ - in twelfths is re-written

$12 \div 6 = 2$ (-common denominator of $12 \div$ denominator of $6 = 2$)

$2 \times 3 = 6$ (-answer 2 x numerator of 3 $= 6$)

so we have: $\frac{3}{6} = \frac{6}{12}$

The sum of $\frac{1}{4} + \frac{3}{6}$ now becomes:

$\frac{3}{12} + \frac{6}{12}$

Since these fractions have the same denominator they can be added together as with the previous example:-

$\frac{3}{12} + \frac{6}{12} = \frac{3+6}{12} = \frac{9}{12}$

So our sum is: $\frac{1}{4} + \frac{3}{6} = \frac{9}{12}$

Subtraction of fractions with different denominators is carried out in exactly the same way.

ITQ 11

Work out the Lowest Common Denominator (LCD) of the following fractions.

1. $\frac{1}{5}$ and $\frac{4}{15}$

LCD = _____

2. $\frac{1}{4}$ and $\frac{2}{3}$

LCD = _____

3. $\frac{9}{16}, \frac{1}{8}$ and $\frac{3}{4}$

LCD = _____

ITQ 12

Calculate the following. Make use of the LCD's found in ITQ 11.

1. $\frac{1}{5} + \frac{4}{15}$

Ans _____

2. $\frac{1}{4} + \frac{2}{3}$

Ans _____

3. $\frac{9}{16} - \frac{1}{8}$

Ans _____

4. $\frac{7}{10} - \frac{1}{5}$

Ans _____

ITQ 13

By finding the lowest common denominator first, work out which of the following fractions is the largest and fill in the corresponding circle. Try to work out the answers 'in your head' as far as possible

1. $\frac{2}{3}$ $\frac{3}{4}$

    O   O

2. $\frac{2}{3}$ $\frac{5}{9}$ $\frac{11}{18}$

   O   O   O

14

3.

$\frac{1}{3}$	$\frac{2}{5}$	$\frac{11}{30}$
O	O	O

4.

$\frac{5}{6}$	$\frac{3}{4}$	$\frac{7}{8}$
O	O	O

Multiplication and Division

Multiplication and division of fractions is straightforward. In order to multiply fractions together all you have to do is multiply the two numerators (top numbers) together, and multiply the two denominators (bottom numbers) together.

e.g. $\frac{1}{5} \times \frac{2}{3} = \frac{1 \times 2}{5 \times 3} = \frac{2}{15}$

So when multiplying fractions together the rule is:

Multiply the two top numbers
Multiply the two bottom no's

ITQ 14

Calculate the following.

1. $\frac{3}{5} \times \frac{4}{6}$

Ans_____

2. $\frac{2}{3} \times \frac{1}{9}$

Ans_____

3. $\frac{4}{15} \times \frac{2}{3}$

Ans_____

4. $\frac{1}{7} \times \frac{2}{9}$

Ans_____

5. $\frac{2}{9} \times \frac{3}{9}$

Ans_____

Division of fractions is similar except the fraction on the right-hand side must be:

(i) turned upside down

(e.g. $\frac{3}{5}$ becomes $\frac{5}{3}$)

(ii) then multiplied with the fraction on the left-hand side.

e.g. $\frac{1}{5} \div \frac{3}{10} = ?$

stage (i) $\frac{3}{10}$ becomes $\frac{10}{3}$

stage (ii) $\frac{1 \times 10}{5 \times 3} = \frac{10}{15}$

i.e. $\frac{1}{5} \div \frac{3}{10} = \frac{10}{15}$

So when dividing fractions the rule is:-

Turn the right-hand fraction upside down and then multiply the two fractions together.

15

ITQ 15

Calculate the following ('in your head' if possible).

1. $\dfrac{1}{6} \div \dfrac{2}{8}$

Ans_____

2. $\dfrac{1}{4} \div \dfrac{5}{9}$

Ans_____

3. $\dfrac{3}{15} \div \dfrac{1}{3}$

Ans_____

4. $\dfrac{2}{7} \div \dfrac{3}{8}$

Ans_____

Cancelling (Equivalent Fractions)

Some fractions can be cancelled so as to express them in smaller numbers. The value of the fraction is not altered by cancelling and so is an 'equivalent fraction'.

For example $\dfrac{4}{6}$ - can be expressed as a fraction having smaller numbers, by dividing BOTH the top and bottom numbers by 2. This is known as cancelling.

i.e. $\dfrac{4 \div 2}{6 \div 2} = \dfrac{2}{3}$

Remember, the value of the fraction has not become smaller, only the numbers involved - this means that $\dfrac{4}{6}$ and $\dfrac{2}{3}$ are equivalent fractions, in other words $\dfrac{4}{6}$ of a piece of cake is the same as $\dfrac{2}{3}$!

Another example of cancelling is $\dfrac{8}{16}$ This can be cancelled three times as follows:

$\dfrac{8}{16}$ can be cancelled to $\dfrac{4}{8}$ by dividing the 8 and the 16 by 2

$\dfrac{8}{16}$ can be cancelled to $\dfrac{2}{4}$ by dividing the 8 and the 16 by 4

$\dfrac{8}{16}$ can be cancelled to $\dfrac{1}{2}$ by dividing the 8 and the 16 by 8

i.e. the equivalent fractions are:-

$$\dfrac{8}{16} = \dfrac{4}{8} = \dfrac{2}{8} = \dfrac{1}{2}$$

If we cancel $\dfrac{8}{16}$ to $\dfrac{1}{2}$ - this is known as cancelling a fraction to its lowest terms (it cannot be reduced any further)

ITQ 16

Cancel the following fractions to their lowest terms.

1. $\frac{3}{6}$ (divide top and bottom by 3)

Ans_____

2. $\frac{15}{20}$ (divide top and bottom by 5)

Ans_____

3. $\frac{12}{36}$

Ans_____

4. $\frac{18}{72}$

Ans_____

5. $\frac{16}{24}$

Ans_____

6. $\frac{14}{16}$

Ans_____

7. $\frac{10}{100}$

Ans_____

8. $\frac{95}{100}$

Ans_____

ITQ 17

Find the missing numbers of these equivalent fractions.

e.g. $\frac{6}{8} = \frac{?}{4}$

(since $4 = 8 \div 2$ then $? = 6 \div 2 = 3$)

Ans 3

1. $\frac{4}{10} = \frac{?}{5}$

Ans_____

2. $\frac{3}{9} = \frac{?}{3}$

Ans_____

3. $\frac{3}{15} = \frac{1}{?}$

Ans_____

4. $\frac{4}{24} = \frac{1}{?}$

Ans_____

RATIOS AND PROPORTIONAL PARTS

RATIOS are similar to fractions and they show how a whole is divided into parts. Examples of ratios are 5:2 (five parts to two parts), 3:1 (three parts to one part), 7:3 (seven parts to four parts). The ratio tells you how many parts in total are present in the whole.

e.g. A ratio of 5:2 means there are 7 parts in the whole (5+2=7),
A ratio of 3:2:6: means there are 11 parts in the whole (3+2+6).

So for a ratio of 5:2 the whole is split into sevenths, and for a ratio of 3:2:6 the whole is split into elevenths.

To find out how much each part of the ratio is of the whole, we divide each part by the total number of parts, i.e. the ratio 5:2 means that the whole is divided into $\frac{5}{7}$ and $\frac{2}{7}$

A ratio of 3:2:6 means that the whole is divided into $\frac{3}{11}$, $\frac{2}{11}$ and $\frac{6}{11}$

This is known as dividing a quantity into proportional parts.

e.g. divide 20 in the ratio of 3:1
1st step: work out the number of parts in the whole, in this case:
3 + 1 = 4 parts in the whole
2nd step: work out the proportional parts (3:1) i.e. 20 is divided into

$\frac{3}{4}$ and $\frac{1}{4}$

3rd step: multiply the whole by the proportional parts

$\frac{3}{4} \times 20^{5} = 15$ (or 3 x 20 ÷ 4 = 15)

$\frac{1}{4} \times 20^{5} = 5$ (or 1 x 20 ÷ 4 = 15)

so 20 in the ratio 3:1 is 15:5

ITQ 18

Divide the following numbers in the ratio stated and write your answers in the boxes provided. Do the working out 'in your head' as far as possible.

1. 40 in the ratio 5:3 is..
(method: $\frac{5}{8}$ x 40 : $\frac{3}{8}$ x 40)

Ans_____:_____

2. 60 in the ratio 5:1 is..

Ans_____:_____

3. 50p in the ratio of 1:4 is..

Ans_____:_____

4. 160 in the ratio 6:2 is

Ans_____:_____

5. 125 in the ration of 19:6 is..

Ans_____:_____

6. 600 in the ratio 3:2:1 is..

Ans_____:_____:_____

18

We will now move on to explain the workings of decimals, which are another way of representing a number which is PART OF A WHOLE.

DECIMALS

HOW can we distinguish a decimal from an ordinary number since decimals use a string of numbers just like any ordinary number? The difference between an ordinary number and a decimal is the DECIMAL POINT. Numbers to the left of the decimal point are whole numbers and those to the right of the point are fractions or parts of a whole.

e.g. 0.25 = nought point two five - note we do not combine the two and the five and say twenty five.

e.g. 1.75 = one point seven five

e.g. 12.36 = twelve point three six

The zero before the point in 0.25 is not essential but is generally left for tidiness, i.e. .25 is normally written 0.25 etc.

Unnecessary and Necessary Zeros

A possible source of confusion when working with decimals is which noughts are needed and which are not.

e.g. 0.3 and 0.300 have exactly the same value but the two zeros after the three are unnecessary, so we would usually write 0.300 as 0.3.

Another example of unnecessary zeros is 0.850, 0.8500, 0.85000 which we would usually write as 0.85.

The following are examples of necessary zeros:-

0.302 and 0.0302, which do not have the same value.

Other examples of necessary zeros are:-

0.507, 0.5007 and 0.50007, which all have different values.

To distinguish between necessary and unnecessary zeros the following rules should be observed when working with decimal fractions:

(1) If there are any numbers greater than zero to the right of a zero or group of zeros then the zero or zeros are necessary.

(2) If there are no numbers greater than zero to the right of a zero or group of zeros then the zero or zeros are unnecessary .

Note: Sometimes unnecessary zeros are purposely left in or included in a sum to help with the calculations. This can be seen in the following section on the addition and subtraction of decimal numbers.

Addition and Subtraction

Addition and subtraction of decimals is exactly the same as for ordinary numbers - the only thing to remember is to keep the decimal points aligned.

e.g. $0.28 + 0.052 + 0.10$

re-write as:-

$$
\begin{array}{l}
0.280 \\
0.052 \\
\underline{0.100}+ \\
\underline{0.432}
\end{array}
$$

- note the points are all under each other

e.g. $0.83 - 0.56$

$$
\begin{array}{l}
0.8\,_13 \quad \text{points are aligned} \\
\underline{0.5\,_16}- \\
\underline{0.2\;7}
\end{array}
$$

Now try the following ITQ (remember to keep the decimal points aligned whenever adding or subtracting decimals).

ITQ 19

Work out the following addition and subtraction sums involving decimals. Try to work out the answers 'in your head as far as you can'.

1. $0.6 + 0.3$

Ans_____

2. $0.86 - 0.5$

Ans_____

3. $0.08 - 0.06$

Ans_____

4. $0.63 + 0.37$

Ans_____

5. $1.135 + 0.006$

Ans_____

6. $1.62 + 1.38$

Ans_____

Multiplication

The process of multiplication of decimals is the same as for the multiplication of ordinary numbers, but there is a further step to work out the position of the decimal point.

Take for example 3.6×5.2

We proceed by working out the sum in the normal way, as if there were no decimal points.

$$
\begin{array}{r}
3.6 \\
\underline{5.2}\times \\
7\,2 \\
\underline{1\,8\,0\,0}+ \\
\underline{1\,8\,7\,2}
\end{array}
$$

So we now have 1872

To find the position of the decimal point:

count the number of numbers to the right of the decimal points (in this case there are two numbers). The decimal point is now moved back this number of places (i.e.) from the right-hand side of the sum to give two decimal places in the answer.

In our example:-

$$\begin{array}{ll} 3.6 & \text{one decimal place} \\ \underline{5.2}x & \text{one decimal place} \\ 7\,2 & \\ \underline{1\,8\,0\,0} & \\ 1\,8.7\,2 & \text{two decimal places} \end{array}$$

i.e. 3.6 x 5.2 = 18.72

and note that:-

no. of decimal places (d.p.'s) in the question = no. of d.p.'s in the answer

another example is 4.21 x 3

$$\begin{array}{lll} \text{i.e.} & 4.2\,1 & \text{two decimal places} \\ & \underline{3}x & \text{no decimal places} \\ & 1\,2.6\,3 & \text{two decimal places} \\ & & \text{in the answer} \end{array}$$

note: when multiplying decimals it is useful to: REMOVE ALL the unnecessary zeros from the numbers you are multiplying together to simplify the workings.

e.g. 10.200 x 0.30

re-write this as 10.2 x 0.3 and then proceed in the normal way.

Work out the following multiplication sums 'in your head' where possible.

1. 3.2 x 5

Ans_____

2. 5.0 x 1.6

Ans_____

3. 1.2 x 12.0

Ans_____

4. 0.09 x 3.1

Ans_____

5. 0.002 x 2.5

Ans_____

6. 9.25 x 4.0

Ans_____

Division

Division of decimals by whole numbers e.g. 6, 13, 25 etc. is carried out as for ordinary numbers and the decimal point remains the same (i.e. is kept in the same vertical row).

For example: 65.25 ÷ 5

$$\begin{array}{l} \quad\;\, 13\,.\,05 \\ 5\,\overline{)\,6^{1}5.2^{2}5} \end{array}$$

21

i.e. $65.25 \div 5 = 13.05$ - no need to move decimal point when dividing

In order to divide any number by a decimal number the decimal MUST first be converted to a whole number (i.e. there must be no numbers to the right of the decimal point). For example, we cannot divide by such numbers as 2.3, 25.7, 0.45 etc. The only way to carry out division by decimals is to multiply the decimal by 10, 100, or 1000 etc., in order to move the decimal point and produce a whole number.

e.g. $4.5 \div 0.3$

1st step: make the 0.3 into a whole number by multiplying it by 10 which gives 3 $(0.3 \times 10 = 3)$

2nd step: multiply the 4.5 by the same amount, i.e. 10 to give 45

$(4.5 \times 10 = 45)$, so $4.5 \div 0.3$ is re-written as $45 \div 3$ and the sum becomes:

$$3\overline{)4^15} \quad \frac{15}{}$$

Another example is: $9 \div 0.15$

1st step: multiply 0.15×100 to give 15

2nd step: multiply 9×100 to give 900 so $0.15 \div 9.00$ is re-written to give

$$15\overline{)900} \quad \frac{60}{}$$

i.e. $9 \div 0.15 = 60$

ITQ 21

Work out the following divisions by decimal numbers (in your head of possible).

1. $3.6 \div 0.6$

Ans_____

2. $6.4 \div 0.4$

Ans_____

3. $66 \div 3.3$

Ans_____

4. $0.55 \div 5.5$

Ans_____

5. $9.99 \div 0.3$

Ans_____

Multiplication by Powers of Ten

i.e. x10 x100 x1000 etc.

Multiplication by multiples (*powers*) of ten can be carried out quickly by simply moving the decimal place to the right. To multiply:

x 10 you move the decimal point (d.p.) 1 place to the right

x 100 you move the d.p. 2 places to the right

x 1000 you move the d.p. 3 places to the right

(i.e. you move the decimal point by the number of noughts you have)

22

examples:

$$0.73 \times 1\underline{0} = 0.7\overset{\curvearrowleft}{3} = 7.3$$
1 jump

$$0.73 \times 1\underline{00} = 0.73 = 73$$
2 jumps

$$0.73 \times 1\underline{000} = 0.730 = 730$$
3 jumps

Division by Powers of 10

Just as in multiplication of decimals, we can divide decimals by powers of ten, i.e. by 10, by 100, by 1000 etc., by moving the decimal point. This is simply the reverse of the multiplication case, i.e. move the DECIMAL POINT to the LEFT.

e.g. $25.34 \div 10 = 2.534$
$\div 100 = 0.2534$
$\div 1000 = 0.02534$

ITQ 22

Work out the following by moving the decimal point by the number of noughts you have.

1. $1.5897 \times 1000 =$
(i.e. move point 3 places to the right)

2. $7692105 \div 10000 =$
(i.e. move point 4 places to the left)

3. $31.729 \times 100 =$

4. $0.175 \div 1000 =$

5. $17.1703 \times 1000 =$

6. $0.0058 \div 100 =$

Squares of Numbers

The square of a number is a number multiplied by itself, and is shown by a small 2 (known as an indice - pronounced "indysee") placed above the number.

e.g. 4^2 (four squared) means 4×4 i.e. $4^2 = 16$
similarly 9^2 (nine squared) means 9×9 i.e. $9^2 = 81$
a larger example is:
$5000^2 = 5000 \times 5000 = 25000000$

Cubes of Numbers

The cube of a number is a number multiplied by itself twice and is shown by a small 3 placed above the number e.g. 2^3 (two cubed) means $2 \times 2 \times 2$ i.e. $2^3 = 8$
similarly 5^3 (five cubed) means $5 \times 5 \times 5$ i.e. $5^3 = 125$

Indices

We have already looked at two types of indices - squares and cubes. Here the index numbers were two and three respectively, however, index numbers can be any size. The small index number (also known as 'a power') tells you how many times you have to multiply the big number by itself.

e.g. 2^4 means $2 \times 2 \times 2 \times 2$ (two to the power four)
7^5 means $7 \times 7 \times 7 \times 7 \times 7$ (seven to the power five)
10^6 means $10 \times 10 \times 10 \times 10 \times 10 \times 10$ (ten to the power six)

Index numbers can also be negative in value. In this case the answer is found as above and then divided into the number one.

e.g. 2^{-4} means $1 \div 2 \times 2 \times 2 \times 2$

7^{-5} means $1 \div 7 \times 7 \times 7 \times 7 \times 7$

Standard Form

By using powers of ten ($10^2, 10^3, 10^4$ etc.,) it is possible to write both large and small numbers in a short form known as 'standard form'. The first step is to re-write the number so that the left-hand figure is placed in the units column and the remaining figures are placed behind the decimal point.

e.g. write 2563 in standard form
1st step: re-write this as 2.563
2nd step: multiply this number by a power of ten so that the re-written number becomes the size of the original number. In this case 2.563 is multiplied by 1000 or 10^3.

i.e. 2563 written in standard form is 2.563×10^3

e.g. write 524000000 in standard form
1st step: re-write as 5.24000000 including the zeros only for ease of working.
2nd step: multiply this number by 100000000 or 10^8 to bring it back to its original size.
i.e. 524000000 in standard form is 5.24×10^8

To be able to use standard form you need to be familiar with multiplying numbers by the index form of ten (or powers of ten) i.e. 10^2, 10^3, 10^4 etc. You also need to be familiar with converting these index forms to single numbers.

The following powers of ten are worth noting. They include negative indices, which are used when dividing by powers of ten:

$10^3 = 1000$ (x10x10x10)

$10^2 = 100$ (x10x10)

$10^1 = 10$ (x10)

$10^{-1} = 0.1$ ($\div 10$)

$10^{-2} = 0.01$ ($\div 100$)

$10^{-3} = 0.001$ ($\div 1000$)

Examples of using powers of 10:

$5 \times 10^3 = 5 \times 1000 = 5000$

$5 \times 10^{-3} = 5 \div 1000 = 0.005$

$1.2 \times 10^6 = 1.2 \times 1000000 = 1200000$

$1.2 \times 10^{-6} = 1.2 \div 1000000 = 0.0000012$

ITQ 23

Complete the following statements

1   $43000000 = 4.3 \times 10^{?}$ ------

2. $0.155 = 155 \times 10^{?}$ ------

Write the following as one number.

3. $25 \times 10^3 =$

4. $3.354 \times 10^{-2} =$

24

THE METRIC SYSTEM OF MEASUREMENT (SI UNITS)

You need to become familiar with basic metric measurements, the most important of which are weight and volume. SI units (international system) are in most cases the same as metric units, all being based on units of ten. The metric system is much easier to understand than the imperial system (pounds, feet, inches etc.)

Weight

The basic unit of weight is the gram (g). All metric weights are based on this. There are 4 weights you are likely to encounter, these are:

Name	Symbol
kilogram	kg
gram	g
milligram	mg

$1 \text{ kg} = 1000 \text{ g}$

and $1 \text{g} = \dfrac{1}{1000}$ th of a kg.

A gram is 1000 milligrams:

$1 \text{ g} = 1000 \text{ mg}$ and

$1 \text{ mg} = \dfrac{1}{1000}$ th of a kg

In some calculations it is necessary to convert from one unit of weight to another, i.e. g to mg, kg to g, etc.

For example, convert 2g to milligrams. Since 1 g = 1000 mg, then to convert g to mg you multiply by 1000. So 2 g in grams is 2 x 1000 = 2000 mg.

Similarly 5.5 kg converted to g is 5.5 x 1000 = 5500 g
(because 1 kg = 1000 g)

Another example is:- convert 2200 mg to grams. This time we divide by 1000 because 1 mg =

$\dfrac{1}{1000}$ th a gram.

So 2200 mg in g is:-

$2200 \div 1000 = 2.2 \text{ g}$

Length

The basic unit of length is the metre (m). All metric lengths are based on this. There are four lengths you may encounter, these are:

Name	Symbol
kilometre	km
metre	m
centimetre	cm
millimetre	mm

A kilometre is 1000 metres.

i.e. 1 km = 1000 m and

$1 \text{ m} = \dfrac{1}{1000}$ th of a km

A metre is 100 centimetres.

1 m = 100 cm and

$1 \text{cm} = \dfrac{1}{100}$ th of a metre

A centimetre is 10 millimetres

1 cm = 10 mm and

$1 \text{mm} = \dfrac{1}{10}$ th of a cm

With this information it is possible to convert from km to m, m to cm, m to mm, m to km etc.

For example:
convert 3 kilometres to metres.

Since 1 km = 1000 metres, then to convert km to m you multiply by 1000. So 3 km in metres is:
3 x 1000 = 3000 m

Similarly, 6.25 metres converted to cm is 6.25 x 100 = 625 cm (because 1 m = 100 cm).

Another example is:-
convert 420 mm to cm.

This time we divide 420 by 10 because 1 mm = $\frac{1}{10}$ th of a centimetre. So 420 mm in centimetres is 420 ÷ 10 = 42 cm.

To convert metres to mm you use two steps, i.e.
 i) convert the metres to centimetres, and then
ii) convert the centimetres (answer from step i) to millimetres.

e.g. convert 0.75m to mm

i) 0.75m = 0.75x 100cm = 75 cm

ii) 75cm = 75 x 10mm = 750 mm

So 0.75 metres expressed in millimetres is 750 mm.

ITQ 24

Complete the following. ALL your answers should be symbols.

1. kilometre is … _____
2. metre is … _____
3. centimetre is … _____
4. millimetre is … _____
5. kilogram is … _____
6. gram is … _____
7. milligram is … _____
8. 1 metre x 1000 = 1… _____
9. 1 centimetre x 100 = 1… _____
10. 1 millimetre x 10 = 1… _____
11. 1 gram x 1000 = 1… _____
12. 1 milligram x 1000 = 1… _____

Convert the following weights and lengths to the units specified.

13. Convert 250 mm to cm
Ans _____ cm

14. Convert 12 km to m
Ans _____ m

15. Convert 100 mg to g
Ans _____ g

16 . Convert 1250 mg to g
Ans _____ g

17. Convert 5.25kg to g
Ans _____ g

Adding and Subtracting Metric Units

When working out sums with metric units it is important that all the numbers have the SAME UNITS. For example, add 2 cm to 1 m. In this case we have to convert either the 2 cm to metres or the 1 metre to centimetres before adding the quantities. Since the answer is going to be bigger than 1 m, we would normally choose metres for the units of the answer, unless told otherwise.

So: $2 \text{ cm} = \frac{2}{100} \text{ m} = 0.02 \text{ m}$ (see also decimal section)

i.e. $1\text{m} + 2\text{cm} = 1\text{m} + 0.02\text{m}$

$$= \begin{array}{r} 1.00 \\ 0.02 + \\ \hline \end{array}$$

Answer: $\underline{1.02}$ metres

(Note: only 1 unit should be used with metric quantities, i.e. a length of 1 metre and 2cm should always be written 1.02m, never 1m 2cm.)

e.g. Work out the following:
1.5 g + 50 mg

We again choose to work in the largest units, - g.

So: $1.5 \text{ g} = 1.5 \text{ g}$

$50 \text{ mg} = \frac{50}{1000} \text{ g} = 0.05 \text{ g}$

To finish the above sum we can now see that adding 1.5 g and 50 mg (0.05 kg) gives:

$$\begin{array}{r} 1.50 \\ 0.05 + \\ \hline \underline{1.55} \text{ g} \end{array}$$

ITQ 25

Work out the following sums involving metric quantities ('in your head if possible').

1. 2 metres 9 cm - 1 metre 3 cm
    (in metres)

    Ans _____m

2. 1 metre 9 cm + 25 mm
    (in centimetres)

    Ans _____cm

3. 1.6 x 250 g (in kg)

    Ans_____kg

4. 2.25 kg + 750 g (in kg)

    Ans_____kg

Volume (Capacity)

Quantities of liquids are measured in litres (l). You are probably familiar with litres through putting petrol in your car; you may also meet the millilitre (ml).

A litre is 1000 millilitres:

$1 \text{ l} = 1000 \text{ ml}$ and

$1 \text{ ml} = \frac{1}{1000}$ th of 1 litre

MENSURATION

Mensuration is concerned primarily with areas and volumes of shapes.

Areas

Areas are measured in units squared (units²) and the metric units of area are square metre (m^2), square centimetre (cm^2) and square millimetre (mm^2).

Area of a Square

The area of a square is given by multiplying its length by its breadth. From the figure below this is given by:

Area = a x a = a^2

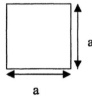

- remember for a square, all the sides are the same length, hence the length is the same as the breadth.

Area of a Rectangle

The area of a rectangle is found by multiplying its length by its breadth, referring to the diagram below, this is given by:

Area = l x b

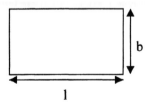

Area of a Triangle

The area of any triangle is found by multiplying half the base by the vertical height:

Area = $\frac{1}{2}$ b x h

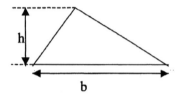

Area of a Circle

Before you can work out the area of any circle, there are a few important pieces of information you need to know about a circle, as shown below:

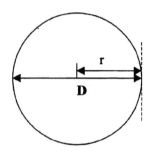

a) The distance from the centre of the circle to the edge is known as the radius (r).

b) The distance from one edge of the circle to the opposite edge going through the centre is known as the diameter (D).

c) The diameter is twice as long as the radius, i.e. D = 2r ; likewise the radius is half as long as the diameter

i.e. $r = \frac{1}{2} D$

d) A relationship exists between the diameter of a circle and its circumference (or perimeter), i.e. the circumference (C) is roughly $3\frac{1}{7}$ or $\frac{22}{7}$ times greater than the diameter,

i.e. $C = \frac{22}{7} \times D$ - This number of $\frac{22}{7}$ was first calculated by the Greeks and given the symbol π (known as 'pi' and pronounced pie.)

The modern figure is more accurate and pi is usually taken to be 3.142 (to three decimal places), although $\frac{22}{7}$ is often used in maths tests.

The area of a circle is given by:
pi multiplied by r multiplied by r,

i.e. Area of a circle $= \pi \times r \times r = \pi\ r^2$

e.g. Find the area of the following circle (take $\pi = \frac{22}{7}$)

28 mm

$r = 0.5 \times D = 14$ mm
$$Area = \pi\ r^2 = \frac{22}{7} \times 14^2 \times 14$$
$$= 22 \times 2 \times 14$$
i.e. area $= 616$ mm^2

ITQ 26

Work out the areas of the following shapes, in the units specified ('in your head').

1.
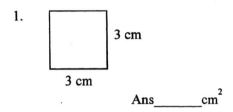
3 cm

3 cm

Ans_____cm^2

2.
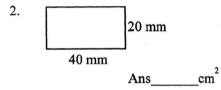
20 mm

40 mm

Ans_____cm^2

3.
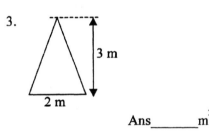
3 m

2 m

Ans_____m^2

4. (take pi $= \frac{22}{7}$)

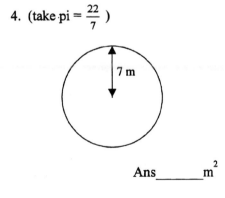
7 m

Ans_____m^2

Perimeters

The perimeter of any shape is the distance all the way round the outside of the shape. We have already met the perimeter of a circle, known as the circumference.

e.g. Find the perimeter of the following square.

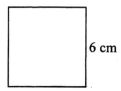

6 cm

The perimeter consists of four 6 cm sides.
i.e. perimeter = 6 + 6 + 6 + 6 = 24 cm

e.g. Find the perimeter of the following rectangle.

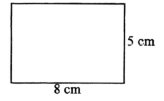

5 cm

8 cm

The perimeter consists of two 5 cm sides and two 8 cm sides.

i.e. perimeter = 5 + 5 + 8 + 8 = 26 cm

e.g. Find the perimeter of the following triangle.

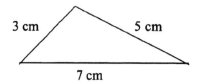

3 cm   5 cm

7 cm

The perimeter consists of one 3 cm side, one 5 cm side and one 7 cm side.

i.e. perimeter = 3 + 5 + 7
= 15 cm

Volumes
Solids

Volume is a measure of the space taken up by a 3-dimensional object. It is measured in units cubed (units^3) and the standard units of volume are the cubic metre (m^3), cubic centimetre (cm^3) and cubic millimetre (mm^3).

The most common solids have a prism shape, which means they have the same cross-section throughout their length - like the examples below:

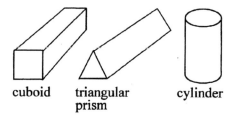

cuboid   triangular   cylinder
          prism

Everyday solids having a prism shape are a book, a plank of wood, a piece of cheese, a door wedge, a tin can, a ten pence piece etc.

The volume of a prism is given by:

Volume (V) = area of its cross-section (end) x its length

30

e.g. Find the volume of the cuboid.

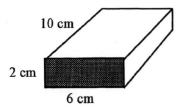

10 cm

2 cm

6 cm

Step (i)   Work out the area of the front face (shaded)

i.e. $6 \times 2 = 12 \text{ cm}^2$

Step (ii)   Multiply the area of the front face by the length of the prism

i.e. $12 \text{ cm}^2 \times 10 \text{ cm} = 120 \text{ cm}^3$
So: volume of the cuboid $= 120 \text{ cm}^3$

Liquids (Capacity)
Volumes of liquids tend to have their own special units - you will already be familiar with pints and gallons, which are 'imperial' units, however, scientific, technical and modern measurements of liquids are made in litres (l) and millilitres (ml), - a millilitre being one thousandth of a litre (as mentioned earlier.

i.e.   1 litre = 1000 ml

One litre is the space inside a cube box which has sides 10 cm in length,

so:- $1 \text{ l} = 10 \times 10 \times 10 \text{ cm} = 1000 \text{ cm}^3$

This means that:-

1 litre $= 1000 \text{ cm}^3 = 1000 \text{ ml}$; and
$1 \text{ cm}^3 = 1 \text{ ml}$

(note: you may also come across cl - a centilitre, which is one tenth of a litre)

ITQ 27

Find the volume of the following shapes in the units specified.

1. in ml

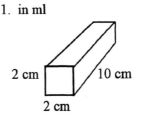

2 cm   10 cm

2 cm

Ans_____ml

2. in litres

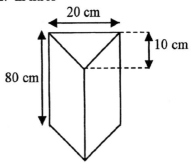

20 cm

10 cm

80 cm

Ans_____l

3. in litres

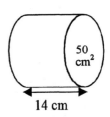

50 cm^2

14 cm

Ans_____l

31

IMPERIAL SYSTEM

THIS is the original British system of measurement, which is still in use alongside the metric system, in the construction industry, manufacturing, engineering and the retail trades. The imperial system of measurements is summarised below.

Weight
16 ounces (oz) = 1 pound (lb)
14 pounds = 1 stone (st)
112 pounds = 1 hundredweight (cwt)
20 hundredweight = 1 ton

Length
12 inches (in, ") = 1 foot (ft ')
e.g. 5 feet 9 inches can be written 5'9"
3 feet = 1 yard (yd)
1760 yards = 1 mile

Area
square inch (in^2)
square foot (ft^2)
square yard (yd^2)

Volume of Solids
cubic inch (in^3)
cubic foot (ft^3)
cubic yard (yd^3)

Capacity (Volume of liquids)
1 pint (pt) = 20 fluid ounces (fl.oz)
2 pints = 1 quart
8 pints = 1 gallon (gal)

Numbers
1 dozen = 12
1 gross = 12 dozen (12 x 12) = 144

ITQ 28

Complete the following.   All your answers should be symbols.

1. The symbol for yards is...
Ans_____

2. The symbol for feet is...
Ans_____or_____

3. The symbol for inches is...
Ans_____or_____

4. The symbol for ounces is...
Ans_____

5. The symbol for pounds is...
Ans_____

6. The symbol for stones is...
Ans_____

7. The symbol for hundred weight is..
Ans_____

8.   1 inch x 12 = ...
Ans 1_____

9.   1 foot x 3 = ...
Ans 1_____

10.   1 yard ÷ 36 = ...
Ans 1_____

11.   1 mile ÷ 1760 = ...
Ans 1

12.   1 ounce x 16 = ...
Ans 1_____

13.   1 pound x 14 = ...
Ans 1_____

14. 1 pound x 112 = ...
Ans 1_____

15. 1 ton ÷ 20 = ...
Ans 1_____

16. 1 fluid ounce x 20 = ...
Ans 1_____

17. 1 pint x 8 = ...
Ans 1_____

ITQ 29

Convert the following weights and lengths to the units specified.

1. Convert 70 inches to feet and inches
Ans_____

2. Convert 360 feet to yards
Ans_____

3. Convert 440 yards to miles
Ans_____

4. Convert 150 lbs to stones and pounds.
Ans_____

5. Convert 30 ounces to pounds and ounces
Ans_____

6. Convert 400 pints to gallons
Ans_____

7. Convert 3 quarts to pints
Ans_____

TIME

CANDIDATES should be aware that:

60 seconds (s) = 1 minute (min);
60 minutes = 1 hour (h,hr);
24 hours = 1 day (d);
28,29,30 or 31 days = 1 month

365 days = 1 year ;
366 days = 1 leap year

13 weeks = 1 quarter;
52 weeks = 1 year;
12 months = 1 year
p.a. = per annum = per year;
a.m. = before noon; p.m. = afternoon
GMT = Greenwich Mean Time

Candidates should be familiar with both the 12 hour clock (which has two 12 hour periods - a.m. and p.m.) and the 24 hour clock, which starts and finishes at midnight, i.e. midnight = 0000 hours and 2400 hours (twenty four hundred hours); noon (midday) = 1200 hrs (twelve hundred hours).

Times can be converted from the 12 hour clock to the 24 hour clock by re-writing the time as a four digit number and adding 12 hours to all p.m. times.

For example:

8.30 a.m. = 0830 hrs (O eight thirty hours)

1 p.m. = 1 + 12 hrs = 1300 hrs (thirteen hundred hours)

10.45 p.m. = 10.45 + 12 hrs = 2245 (twenty-two forty-five hours)

Likewise, times on the 24 hour clock can be converted to 12 hour clock times by subtracting 12 hours from all afternoon times (i.e. those greater than 1200 hrs).

For example:-

2050 hours = 2050 -12 hrs = 8.50 pm

SPEED, DISTANCE AND TIME

SPEED, or more precisely, average speed (i.e. the 'overall speed') can be calculated by dividing the distance travelled by the time taken.

i.e. Speed = Distance ÷ Time

Example: If it takes a car 2 hours to travel 100 miles, what is its average speed?

$$Speed = \frac{Distance}{Time}$$

$$Speed = \frac{100\ miles}{2\ hours}$$

= 50 miles per hour (50 mph)

Example: A man walks 12 kilometres in 3 hours. Calculate his average speed.

$$Speed = \frac{Distance}{Time}$$

$$Speed = \frac{12\ km}{3\ hrs}$$

= 4 kilometres per hour (4 kmh)

ITQ 30

1. An aeroplane flew 6 hours before reaching its destination. If it covered 3000 miles, what was its average speed?

Ans_____mph

2. A train leaves London at 0915 hrs and arrives in Glasgow at 1345 hrs. If the distance travelled is 630 km, calculate the average speed.

Ans_____kmh

3. A man jogs at 12 km/hr along a country lane. How far will he travel in 1 hour 30 minutes?

Ans_____km

4. A woman takes a 2 mile bus ride to work at 0800 hrs. If the bus travels at an average speed of 20 mph, at what *time* will she arrive?

(hint: $\frac{2}{0.1} = 20$)

Ans_____hrs

34

TEMPERATURE

THIS is measured in either degrees Fahrenheit (°F) or in degrees Celsius (°C). Temperatures can be converted from one temperature scale to another as follows:

$°C = (°F - 32) \times \frac{5}{9}$ (degrees Celsius from degrees Fahrenheit)

$°F = °C \times \frac{9}{5} + 32$ (degrees Fahrenheit from degrees Celsius)

e.g. What is 50°F in degrees Celsius?

$°C = (°F - 32) \times \frac{5}{9}$

$°C = (50 - 32) \times \frac{5}{9}$

$= 18 \times \frac{5}{9}$

$= 10°C$

e.g. What is 25°C in degrees Fahrenheit?

$°F = °C \times \frac{9}{5} + 32$

$°F = 25 \times \frac{9}{5} + 32$

$= 45 °F + 32$

$= 77°F$

ITQ 31

1. By how many degrees Celsius does the temperature rise from -7°C to +10°C?

Ans _____°C

2. If normal body temperature is 98.6°F, what is normal body temperature in °C?

Ans _____°C

MONEY

SOME questions involve money matters so candidates should be familiar with the decimal system of money and the symbols used.

So, for example:-
five pounds = £5
ten pence = 10p
and 1 pound = 100 pence

Because £1 = 100p, all sums of money can be written as decimals, with a point separating the pounds from the pence columns. So for example, five pounds can be written as £5.00; three pounds and twenty pence as £3.20; eighteen pounds and five pence is written £18.05 (there are always two columns for the pence figures). A letter p is not used in amounts which contain pounds so, for example, ten pounds and fifty pence is written as £10.50 and NOT £10.50p.

To convert pounds to pence we multiply by 100 and to convert pence to pounds we divide by 100, so:

£2.50 = 250p (simply move the point 2 places to the right)
and 135p = £1.35 (move the point 2 places to the left)

Also note that:
£0.75 = 0.75 x 100p = 75p
£0.50 = 0.5 x 100p = 50p
£0.05 = 0.05 x 100p = 5p   etc.

We can add and subtract money by writing each amount in the same form, i.e. as either pounds or pence.

So for example:

£1.75 + 90p is re-written:
£1.75 + £0.90 (dividing 90p by 100 to make £0.90's)

i.e. 1.75
    0.90 +
    2.65

Ans £2.65

Similarly: £0.45 - 20p
is rewritten 45p - 20p
= 25p (giving the answer in pence)

Now try the following question on coinage analysis.

ITQ 32

Make up the amounts given using the least number of coins. The first amount has been done for you.

Coins Amount	£1	50p	20p	10p	5p	2p	1p
22p			1				2
45p							
63p							
77p							
99p							
£1.74							
£2.65							
£3.79							
£4.50							
£5.94							

Exchange Rates

Many other countries use a decimal system of currency, similar to our own.

France: 1 franc (Ff) = 100 centimes
Spain: 1 peseta (ptas) = 100 cents
USA: 1 dollar = 100 cents
Germany: 1 Deutschmark (DM) = 100 pfennigs

Pounds can be exchanged for the currency of another country by referring to the exchange rate. Up-to-date exchange rates are displayed in banks and in the financial pages of newspapers. The exchange rate shows how many units of foreign currency can be exchanged (or bought) for one pound. Examples are given below: (note these rates vary from day to day).

France: 9.00 francs (Ff) = £1
Germany: 2.75 Deutschmarks (DM) = £1
Spain: 230 pesatas (ptas) = £1
U.S.A.: 1.62 dollars ($) = £1
Switzerland: 2.27 francs (SF) = £1

e.g. If £100 is exchanged for French francs and the exchange rate is £1 = 9.00 Ff, how many francs will be received?
Ans: If £1 = 8.00 Ff
then £100 = 100 x 9.00 Ff
        = 900 francs

e.g. £1000 is changed to German marks at a rate of £1 = 2.75 DM.
How many marks will be received?
Ans:
£1 = 2.75 DM so £500 = 1000 x 2.75 DM
= 2750 marks

36

Foreign currency can be converted back to English money using the same exchange rates.

e.g. 2000 French francs are exchanged for pounds at a rate of £1 = 8.00 Ff. How many pounds will be received?

Ans: £1 = 8.00 Ff, i.e. 8.00 Ff = £1
so: 2000 Ff = 2000 ÷ 8 pounds
                    = £250

e.g. If 500 German marks are exchanged for English money, how much will be received to the nearest penny if the exchange rate is £1 = 2.5 DM

Ans: £1 = 2.5 DM, i.e. 2.5 DM = £1
So: 500 DM = 500 ÷ 2.5 pounds
                    = £200

Note: If you find it difficult to decide whether to multiply or divide by the exchange rate when converting currencies, then you should check to see whether you get more or less than 1 unit of foreign currency for 1 pound.

e.g. If £1 = 8.00 Ff and £1 = 2.5 DM - you should always get more francs than pounds and more Deutschmarks than pounds, when converting pounds to either of these currencies; likewise you get less pounds than francs or marks when converting these two currencies back to pounds. This applies to most other countries, including Spain, Belgium, Portugal, USA, Canada, Australia, Austria, Switzerland, Greece, Denmark, Norway, Sweden, Holland, Italy,

Turkey, South Africa, Japan and Hong Kong - i.e. you get more units of foreign currency than you have pounds when changing pounds (exceptions are Malta and Cyprus).

ITQ 33

1. If 250 pesetas can be exchanged for £1, then:-

a) how many pesetas can be exchanged for £100?
                                          Ans_____

b) how many pounds can be exchanged for 1000 pesetas?
                                          Ans_____

2. An American tourist bought a watch for £50. How many dollars is this at an exchange rate of £1 = $1.60?

                                          Ans_____

3. A British tourist spent 200 Francs on duty free goods. How many pounds is this at an exchange rate of £1 = 8 francs?

                                          Ans_____

4. How much more money, in pounds, is 7500 pesetas compared with $32 (use the exchange rates in questions 1 and 2).

                                          Ans_____

PERCENTAGES

A percentage (percentage sign = %) means 'out of a hundred' in other words something is spit into a hundred equal parts and each one part is one percent. A percentage is basically a special case of a fraction. ALL percentage fractions have the same bottom number which is on hundred. All that changes is the top number.

e.g. $3\% = \dfrac{3}{100}$ $(3 \div 100)$

$95\% = \dfrac{95}{100} = \dfrac{19}{20}$ (by cancellng)

Percentages can also be written in decimal form. To do this we divide the percentage by 100, expressing the answer as a decimal. The easiest way to divide by 100 is to move the decimal point two places to the left.

e.g. Express 50% as a decimal.

Ans: $50.0 \div 100 = 0.5$

Similarly, 15% as a decimal:

Ans: $15.0 \div 100 = 0.15$

Similarly, 5% as a decimal:

Ans: $05.0 \div 100 = 0.05$

ITQ 34

Convert the following percentages to fractions and decimals.. The first question has been done for you.

1. 20%
Fraction: $\dfrac{20}{100} = \dfrac{1}{5}$ Decimal: = 0.2

2. 25%
Fraction: Decimal:

3. 10%
Fraction: Decimal:

4. 75%
Fraction: Decimal:

5. 90%
Fraction: Decimal:

6. 45%
Fraction: Decimal:

7. 35%
Fraction: Decimal:

8. 22%
Fraction: Decimal:

9. 2%
Fraction: Decimal:

10. 4%
Fraction: Decimal:

11. 12.5% (hint: see also question 2)
Fraction: Decimal:

12. 37.5%
Fraction: Decimal:

38

How do you work out the percentage of something? To do this you must multiply the "something" by the percentage.

e.g. Find 25% of 60

25% = 25 ÷ 100 = 0.25

then 0.25 x 60 = **15**

Another method is to convert the percentage to a fraction.

e.g. Find 25% of 60

$25\% = \dfrac{25}{100} = \dfrac{1}{4}$

$\dfrac{1}{4} \times 60 = \textbf{15}$

In the above example, the fraction method of working out percentage is easier than the decimal method but in some cases the reverse is true, this is why it is good practise to be able to use both methods competently.

ITQ 35

Work out the following percentages using either the fractions method (questions 1 to 4) or the decimal method (questions 5 to 8).

Use the fractions method:

1. 50% of 175

Ans_____

2. 30% of 200

Ans_____

3. 20% of 300

Ans_____

4. 15% of 120

Ans_____

Use the decimal method:

5. 62.5% of 200

Ans_____

6. $72\dfrac{1}{2}$% of 400

Ans_____

7. $12\dfrac{1}{2}$% of 500

Ans_____

8. $2\dfrac{1}{2}$% of 1000

Ans_____

9. If 90% of applicants fail to become police officers what percentage are successful?

Ans____%

10. There are 1200 applicants per week. How many will become police officers?

Ans_____

Expressing Whole Numbers, Fractions and Decimals, as Percentages.

We have seen that percentage means out of 100, so:

$$100\% = \frac{100}{100} = 1$$

This means that we can write any number as a percentage, without affecting its value, by multiplying it by 100 %, i.e. by 1.

So, for example:
2 x 100% = 200%   (i.e. 2 wholes is 200%)

10 x 100% = 1000% (i.e. 10 wholes is 1000%)

Consider the following examples:

6 x 200% = 6 x 2 = 12

25 x 1000% = 25 x 10 = 250

200 x 150% = 20 x 1.5 = 30

Fractions can be converted to percentages in the same way:

$$\frac{1}{4} \times 100\% = 25\%$$

$$\frac{1}{5} \times 100\% = 20\%$$

$$\frac{1}{10} \times 100\% = 10\%$$

Candidates should be familiar with the above fractions and their equiv-

-valent percentages, so if asked for example, to find 75% of 16, this would be immediately worked out as:

$$\frac{3}{4} \times 16 = 12$$

Decimals fractions can be converted to percentages in the same way, i.e. by multiplying by 100%. For example:

0.15 x 100% = 15%

0.01 x 100% = 1%

0.995 x 100% = 95.5%

ITQ 36

Express the following numbers as percentages by multiplying them by 100%.

1. $\dfrac{17}{20}$

Ans_____%

2. $\dfrac{9}{25}$

Ans_____%

3. 0.22

Ans_____%

4. 0.015

Ans_____%

5. 1.05

Ans_____%

6. 3.2

Ans_____%

Working out Percentages from the Original Number.

Sometimes you will have to work out the percentage from the original figure:

e.g. If a car depreciates by £1000 in its first year and the new cost was £5000, find the depreciation in terms of the original cost.
Answer: It depreciates by £1000, so:

$$\% \text{ depreciation} = \frac{\text{depreciation}}{\text{original cost}} \times 100\%$$

$$\% \text{ depreciation} = \frac{1000}{5000} \times 100\%$$

$$= 20\% \text{ (after cancelling)}$$

e.g. Find the percentage increase in speed when going from 60 to 75 mph.
Answer:
Increase in speed = 75 - 60 = 15 mph

$$\% \text{ increase} = \frac{\text{increase in speed}}{\text{original speed}} \times 100\%$$

$$\% \text{ increase} = \frac{15}{60} \times 100\%$$

$$= 25\%$$

e.g. Find the percentage decrease in speed when slowing down from 75 to 60 mph.
Answer:
Decrease in speed = 75 - 60 = 15 mph

$$\% \text{ decrease} = \frac{\text{decrease in speed}}{\text{original speed}} \times 100\%$$

$$\% \text{ increase} = \frac{15}{75} \times 100\%$$

$$= 20\%$$

e.g. Find the percentage profit if a shop buys a television for £150 and sells it for £200.
Answer:
Profit on sale = 200 - 150 = 50

$$\% \text{ profit} = \frac{\text{profit made}}{\text{cost price}} \times 100\%$$

$$\% \text{ profit} = \frac{50}{150} \times 100\%$$

$$= 33.3\% \text{ (one third)}$$

e.g. Find the percentage loss if a car is bought for £2500 and sold for £1500.
Answer:
Loss on sale = 2500 - 1500 = 1000

$$\% \text{ loss} = \frac{\text{loss made}}{\text{original price}} \times 100\%$$

$$\% \text{ loss} = \frac{1000}{2500} \times 100\%$$

$$= 40\% \text{ (after cancelling)}$$

41

From the five alternatives, choose ONE which best completes the statement and fill in the circle.

1. 100 to 150 is a percentage change of...

33.3%	50%	67%	75%	100%
O	O	O	O	O

2. 50 to 30 is a percentage change of...

20%	40%	60%	67%	70%
O	O	O	O	O

3. 125 to 25 is a percentage change of...

67%	70%	80%	83%	90%
O	O	O	O	O

4. 90 to 100 is a percentage change of...

9%	9.5%	10%	10.5%	11%
O	O	O	O	O

INTEREST

THIS is a special application of percentages and will be considered as a separate topic.

Simple Interest

Simple interest (SI) is interest paid on money (the *principal*) at regular, usually yearly intervals, known as per annum (p.a.). The amount of interest paid each year remains the same.

e.g. Find the simple interest paid on £500 at 10% p.a. after one year.

$$\frac{1}{10} \times 500 = £50$$

e.g. Find the total interest paid on savings of £300 at 12% p.a. simple interest for five years. Hence find the total amount of savings and interest (or new capital).

$$\frac{12}{100} \times 300 = £36$$

So after 5 years:-
Total SI = 5 x £36 = £210

New capital (balance of the account)
= principal + total S.I.
= £300 + £210
= £510

ITQ 38

Work out the following ('in your head if possible'):

i) The total amount of simple interest after the total number of years.

ii) The total amount of savings after the total number of years.

1. initial amount (principal) = £300
   SI = 5%   period = 2 years

Ans i)£_____   Ans ii)£_____

2. Principal = £500
   SI = 8%   period = 3 years

Ans i) £_____ Ans ii) £_____

42

Hire Purchase

You will be familiar with hire purchase (HP) for the purchasing of expensive items such as a car, stereo or a suite of furniture etc. But how much do you actually pay and how much of the repayments is actually interest?

e.g. A suite of furniture costs £900 cash price. If you decide to buy it on HP you have put a one-third deposit down and pay the remainder over 12 months at 15% p.a.

What is:-
i) the total interest payable?
ii) the monthly repayment?
iii) the total cost of the suite?

Answer:
Deposit = one-third of cash price

$$= \frac{1}{3} \times 900 = £300$$

Amount outstanding
= price - deposit
= 900 - 300
= £600

So:-
i) Tot. interest payable
= 15% x £600

$$= \frac{15}{100} \times 600$$

= £90

ii) monthly repayment =

£600 (capital outst.) + £90 (interest)
12 (months)

= 690 ÷ 12 = £57.50

iii) total cost of suite:-

= 300 + 600 + 90 (price + interest)

ITQ 39

Work out the following:

i) the total interest payable
ii) the monthly repayment
iii) the total cost, in the following example.

1. Cash price = £800
   25% Deposit
   Remainder paid over 2 years at
   20% p.a.

Deposit ⟶ Remainder ⟶ Interest
⟶ Monthly repayment

i)

ii)

iii)

43

GRAPHS

THERE are three basic type of graph (chart) you should be familiar with i.e. Bar charts; Pie charts; Line graphs.

Bar Charts

A bar chart is a series of either vertical or horizontal bars which represent or show data. The longer the bar the greater the amount of that particular piece of data, and obviously the shorter the bar the smaller the amount. Bar charts can consist of bars separated by gaps, for individual pieces of data which are unrelated, such as colours, days of the week, etc. They can also consist of bars which are joined together, usually for data which occurs in groups such as age ranges for example 11-20, 21-30, 31-40, 41-50, 51-60. Such bar charts are known as histograms.

The bar chart below compares the prison populations of European countries. To read-off the data, (number of prisoners per million population) you read down from the end of each bar to the number on the value line (x-axis). So, for example, Greece has the lowest rate per million and Portugal the highest rate per million.

ITQ 40

From the horizontal bar chart:
1. What is the prison population in Great Britain per million people?
                                        Ans_____

2. If the population of Great Britain is about 50 million people, about how many thousand prisoners are there?
                                        Ans_____

Prison Populations

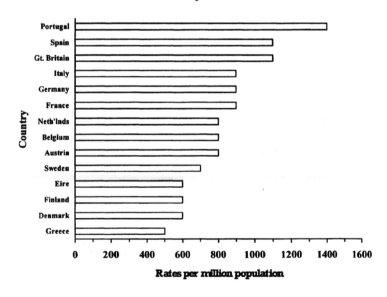

44

Pie Charts

A pie chart shows the comparative size of component parts. It consists of a circle which is divided into various sectors (like pieces of a pie). The larger the sector the greater the number in that particular group. The full circle represent 100% of the data. A typical example is shown on the next page. The size of each sector is shown as a percentage (%) of the full circle.

From the pie chart, we can see that most offenders are fined for motoring offences (59%). Roughly the same number of people receive a custodial sentence as a community one.

To calculate the actual numbers in each sector we need to know the value of the whole data. So, if the total number of people sentenced for motoring offences is 10,000 we can calculate how many people are in each sector.

To do this, we multiply the percentage for each sector by the total members of offenders (10,000).

Fined = 59% x 10,000
i.e. 59 ÷ 100 x 10000 = 5900
Community = 18 % of 10000
18 ÷ 100 x 10000 = 1800
Custody = 15% of 3000
15 ÷ 100 x 10000 = 1500

Type of sentence for motoring offences

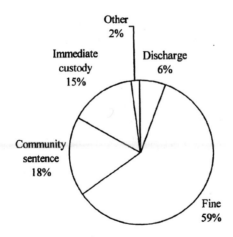

ITQ 41

1. Reading from the pie chart, how many offenders are discharged?

Ans_____

45

Line Graphs

These are just points which are joined together. The advantage of such graphs is that they show variations or fluctuations in data quite easily.

The chart shown below shows how the percentage of offenders varies with age and gender. The highest level of offending is by men aged 18.

ITQ 42

Reading from the graph below. What is the peak age of offending for females?

Age_____

Line graphs to show percentage of offenders (i.e. people found guilty or cautioned for inditable offences) versus age & gender

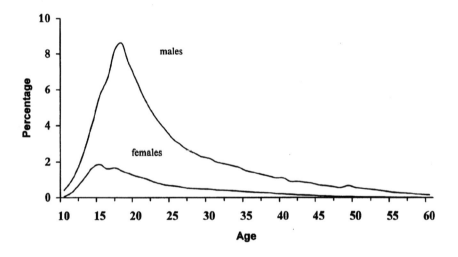

EXAM TECHNIQUES

IN this section we will be reviewing exam techniques and topics that will help you to achieve a higher mark in the examination.

Comprehension of Questions (Key Words)

In the test, you will need to comprehend the question before you start to work out the 'mathematics' of the sum. In other words you have to be able to read the question and sort out exactly what mathematical processes/skills are required. To do this you will need to identify the key words in the question, so that you will know what particular type of calculation is required (i.e. multiplic-ation, division, addition or subtraction etc.).

e.g. If a man buys 50 items which cost 30p each, how much do they cost in total?

In this example, the key words are underlined showing that this sum is a multiplication sum.

The next two examples show how the same type of problem can be put in different ways:-

A library has 759 books. If 215 are borrowed one day, and the next day 123 are returned, how many books does the library contain?

Maths content: subtracting and adding

i.e. 759 - 215 + 123

A boy has 25 marbles. If he loses 6 in one game and wins 13 in another, how many marbles does he have?

Maths content: subtracting and adding

i.e. 25 - 6 + 13

Notice that both of the previous questions involve addition and subtraction, but the non-key words make the questions appear different. Although these examples are fairly simple, the same type of reasoning can be applied to any level of exam question.

Most people experience some difficulty with more detailed or worded questions because their comprehension or understanding of questions needs developing - this problem can be overcome by simplifying or breaking down any question into purely mathematical content, cutting out all the unnecessary words.

For example, if something costs, say 50p, it doesn't matter whether it is bananas, apples or a newspaper - the main thing is the cost. This means that most of the words of phrases used are totally irrelevant to the mathematical content of the sum.

In the questions on the next page, the mathematical content has been separated from the text. Be sure that you can see how the maths content was arrived out from the words used in the question.

Sample Question	**Mathematical Content**
Calculate the cost of a night out if drinks cost £15, the cinema costs £10 and a taxi costs £5.	Adding (whole numbers) i.e. £15 + £10 + £5
How much change should be received if £15 of petrol is paid for with a £20 note?	Subtracting i.e. £20 -£15
Find the cost of 15 gallons of petrol at £3 per gallon.	Multiplying i.e. 15x3 £'s
How many fives are there in 30?	Dividing i.e. 30 ÷ 5
£40 was paid for 8 hours work. How much was this per hour?	Dividing i.e. 40 ÷ 5 £'s
What is the total weight of two bunches of bananas weighing 1.6 kg and 0.5 kg?	Adding (decimal numbers) i.e. 1.6 + 0.5
How much money is left if £198.50 is spent out of a salary of £375.90?	Subtracting (decimals) i.e. 375.9 -198.5
An appliance uses 1000 units of electricity at 9.5p per unit. Calculate the cost in pounds.	Multiplying (decimals) i.e. 1000 x 9.5p Dividing by 100 i.e. 9500 ÷ 100 £'s
If three tickets to a test match cost £54.66, how much does 1 ticket cost?	Dividing (decimals) i.e. 54.66 ÷ 3 £'s
How long will a journey take if it takes half an hour to walk to the bus stop and three quarters of an hour on the bus?	Adding (fractions) $\frac{1}{2} + \frac{3}{4}$
Half a pint of milk is knocked over and one-third of a pint spills out. How much milk remains?	Subtracting (fractions) $\frac{1}{2} - \frac{1}{3}$
Three quarters of a cake is divided into sixths. What fraction of the whole cake will one of the sixths be?	Multiplying (fractions) $\frac{3}{4} \times \frac{1}{6}$

Sample Question	Mathematical Content
How many sixteenths are there in two and a half? (hint: two and a half is: two wholes + one half)	Dividing (fractions) $\dfrac{5}{2} \times \dfrac{16}{1}$
A serving of chips weighs approximately 110g. Roughly how many servings can be made per killogram of potatoes?	Conversion of metric units i.e. $1000 \div 110$
A lift will take a maximum of 1540 lb. How many people of average weight 10 st is this?	Conversion of imperial units i.e. $1540 \div (10 \times 14)$
6 p.m. expressed in terms of the 24 hour clock is ..... hours	Reading the 24 hour clock (adding 12 hours to p.m. times and writing as '000'hrs)
In three time trials, a man runs 100 metres in 10.3s, 10.6s and 10.3s. What is his average time?	Calculate averages i.e. $(10.3 + 10.6 + 10.3) \div 3$
A pair of trousers normally cost £30. If the price is reduced by 30% in a sale, how much will they cost?	Calculate percentages i.e. £30 x 70% or £30 - (£30 x 30%)
Find the interest charged on £500 borrowed for 2 years at 5% above base rate, if the base rate is 8%	Calculate interest i.e. £500 x 13% x 2
A man is charged £66 for 3 nights B&B. How much will he pay for a full week?	i.e. $66 \times \dfrac{7}{3}$
Brass is made from 7 parts zinc and 12 parts copper. How much copper is used to make 95 kg of brass?	Proportions i.e. $7 + 12 = 19$ $\dfrac{12}{19} \times 95 \text{ kg}$
How many square tiles of side 6" are needed to cover a floor 9 feet long and 5 feet wide?	Areas i.e. $(9 \times 5) \div (\dfrac{1}{2} \times \dfrac{1}{2})$ $(= 45 \div \dfrac{1}{4} = 45 \times 4)$

Sample Question	**Mathematical Content**
How many dice of side 20 mm can be packed into a box measuring 15 cm x 10 cm x 6 cm?	Volumes i.e. $\dfrac{15 \times 10 \times 6}{2 \times 2 \times 2}$ (use cancelling)
A car travels at an average speed of 70 kmh. How long does it take to cover 175 km?	Speed, distance and time i.e. $175 \div 70$ hours ($D = S \times T$)
A man walks 2 miles in 40 minutes. What is his average speed in miles per hour?	Speed, distance and time i.e. $2 \div {}^{40}/_{60}$ (3 mph) ($S = D \div T$)
A boy cycles at a speed of 12 miles per hour. How long will it take him to travel 25 miles?	Speed, distance and time i.e. $25 \div 12$ (2 hours 5 min) ($T = D \div S$)
It takes 5 hours to do a certain journey at an average speed of 40 mph. How long will it take at 50 mph?	Ratios (inverse) More speed so less time 5 hours x $^4/_5$ (4 hours)
If £1 = 3 Swiss Francs and 1 Swiss Franc = 3 French Francs, how many French Francs are there to the Pound?	Ratios (foreign currency) Take out the words: £1 = 3 SF; 1SF = 3 FF so £1 = 3 (3FF) = 9FF

Answers to ITQ's

ITQ 1
1. 1168
2. 9042
3. 1009

ITQ 2
1. 14
2. 86
3. 110
4. 433
5. 18050

ITQ 3
1. 2
2. 44
3. 27
4. 100
5. 1127
6. 1112

ITQ 4
1. 12
2. 92
3. 450
4. 95
5. 99

ITQ 5
1. 806
2. 2528
3. 1200
4. 5080

ITQ 6
1. 4
2. 62
3. 113
4. 53

ITQ 7
1. 30
2. 31
3. 44
4. 45
5. 20

ITQ 8
1. 3
2. 5
3. 30

ITQ 9
1. 28
2. 16
3. 20
4. 235

ITQ 10
1. $\frac{7}{8}$
2. $\frac{4}{6}$
3. $\frac{4}{10}$

ITQ 11
1. 15
2. 12
3. 16

ITQ 12
1. $\frac{7}{15}$
2. $\frac{11}{12}$
3. $\frac{7}{16}$
4. $\frac{5}{10}$

ITQ13
1. ○ ●
2. ● ○ ○
3. ○ ● ○
4. ○ ○ ●

ITQ 14
1. $\frac{12}{30}$
2. $\frac{2}{27}$
3. $\frac{8}{45}$
4. $\frac{2}{63}$
5. $\frac{6}{81}$

ITQ15
1. $\frac{8}{12}$
2. $\frac{9}{20}$
3. $\frac{9}{15}$
4. $\frac{16}{21}$

ITQ 16
1. $\frac{1}{2}$
2. $\frac{3}{4}$
3. $\frac{1}{3}$
4. $\frac{1}{4}$

(contd.)

5. $\dfrac{2}{3}$

6. $\dfrac{7}{8}$

7. $\dfrac{1}{10}$

8. $\dfrac{19}{20}$

ITQ17
1. 2
2. 1
3. 5
4. 6

ITQ 18
1. 25:15
2. 50:10
3. 10p:40p
4. 120:40
5. 95:30
6. 300:200:100

ITQ 19
1. 0.9
2. 0.36
3. 0.02
4. 1.00
5. 1.141
6. 3.00

ITQ 20
1. 16
2. 8
3. 14.4
4. 0.279
5. 0.005
6. 37

ITQ 21
1. 6
2. 16
3. 20
4. 0.1
5. 33.3

ITQ 22
1. 1589.7
2. 769.2105
3. 3172.9
4. 0.000175
5. 17170.3
6. 0.000058

ITQ 23
1. 7
2. -3
3. 25000
4. 0.03354

ITQ 24
1. km
2. m
3. cm
4. mm
5. kg
6. g
7. mg
8. km
9. m
10. cm
11. kg
12. g
13. 25
14. 12000
15. 0.1
16. 1.25
17. 5250

ITQ 25
1. 1.06m
2. 111.5cm
3. 0.4kg
4. 3kg

ITQ 26
1. $9cm^2$
2. $8cm^2$
3. $3m^2$
4. $154m^2$

ITQ 27
1. 40 ml
2. 8 1
3. 0.7 1

ITQ 28
1. yd
2. ft or '
3. in or "
4. oz
5. lb
6. st
7. cwt
8. 1 ft
9. 1 yd
10. 1 in or 1"
11. 1 yd
12. 1 lb
13. 1 st
14. 1 cwt
15. 1cwt
16. 1 pt
17. 1 gal

ITQ 29
1. 5'10"
2. 120yd
3. $\frac{1}{4}$ mile
4. 10st 10lb
5. 1 lb 14 oz
6. 50 gal
7. 6pt

ITQ 30
1. 500 mph
2. 140 Kmh
3. 18 km
4. 0806

ITQ 31
1. 17°
2. 37°C

ITQ 32

Coins \ Amount	£1	50p	20p	10p	5p	2p	1p
22p			1				2
45p			2	1			
63p		1		1		1	1
77p		1	1		1	1	
99p		1	2		1	2	
£1.74	1	1	1			2	
£2.65	2	1		1	1		
£3.79	3	1	1		1	2	
£4.50	4	1					
£5.94	5	1	2			2	

ITQ 33
1. (a) 25000 (b) £4
2. $80
3. £25
4. £10

ITQ 34
1. $\frac{1}{5}$ 0.2
2. $\frac{1}{4}$ 0.25
3. $\frac{1}{10}$ 0.1
4. $\frac{3}{4}$ 0.75
5. $\frac{9}{10}$ 0.9
6. $\frac{9}{20}$ 0.45
7. $\frac{7}{20}$ 0.35
8. $\frac{11}{50}$ 0.22
9. $\frac{1}{50}$ 0.02
10. $\frac{2}{25}$ 0.04
11. $\frac{1}{8}$ 0.125
12. $\frac{3}{8}$ 0.375

ITQ 35
1. $87\frac{1}{2}$
2. 60
3. 60
4. 18
5. 125
6. 290
7. 62.5
8. 25
9. 10%
10. 120

ITQ 36
1. 85%
2. 36%
3. 22%
4. 1.5%
5. 105%
6. 320%

ITQ 37
1. 100 to 150 is a percentage change of...

33.3%	50%	67%	75%	100%
O	●	O	O	O

2. 50 to 30 is a percentage change of...

20%	40%	60%	67%	70%
O	●	O	O	O

3. 125 to 25 is a percentage change of...

67%	70%	80%	83%	90%
O	O	●	O	O

4. 90 to 100 is a percentage change of...

9%	9.5%	10%	10.5%	11%
O	O	O	O	●

ITQ 38
1. £30   £330
2. £120   £620

ITQ 39
1. (i) £240   (ii) £35   (iii) £1040

ITQ 40
1. 1100
2. 55000

ITQ 41
1. 600 (6% of 10000)

ITQ 42
1. 15 years

Mock
Test Paper

TIME ALLOWED = 1 HOUR

C J Tyreman

ELC Publications

STOP

Please detach your answer
record sheet NOW

Test 1 - Verbal Usage	
1 Ⓐ Ⓑ Ⓒ Ⓓ Ⓔ	31 Ⓐ Ⓑ Ⓒ Ⓓ Ⓔ
2 Ⓐ Ⓑ Ⓒ Ⓓ Ⓔ	32 Ⓐ Ⓑ Ⓒ Ⓓ Ⓔ
3 Ⓐ Ⓑ Ⓒ Ⓓ Ⓔ	33 Ⓐ Ⓑ Ⓒ Ⓓ Ⓔ
4 Ⓐ Ⓑ Ⓒ Ⓓ Ⓔ	34 Ⓐ Ⓑ Ⓒ Ⓓ Ⓔ
5 Ⓐ Ⓑ Ⓒ Ⓓ Ⓔ	35 Ⓐ Ⓑ Ⓒ Ⓓ Ⓔ
6 Ⓐ Ⓑ Ⓒ Ⓓ Ⓔ	36 Ⓐ Ⓑ Ⓒ Ⓓ Ⓔ
7 Ⓐ Ⓑ Ⓒ Ⓓ Ⓔ	37 Ⓐ Ⓑ Ⓒ Ⓓ Ⓔ
8 Ⓐ Ⓑ Ⓒ Ⓓ Ⓔ	38 Ⓐ Ⓑ Ⓒ Ⓓ Ⓔ
9 Ⓐ Ⓑ Ⓒ Ⓓ Ⓔ	39 Ⓐ Ⓑ Ⓒ Ⓓ Ⓔ
10 Ⓐ Ⓑ Ⓒ Ⓓ Ⓔ	40 Ⓐ Ⓑ Ⓒ Ⓓ Ⓔ
11 Ⓐ Ⓑ Ⓒ Ⓓ Ⓔ	41 Ⓐ Ⓑ Ⓒ Ⓓ Ⓔ
12 Ⓐ Ⓑ Ⓒ Ⓓ Ⓔ	42 Ⓐ Ⓑ Ⓒ Ⓓ Ⓔ
13 Ⓐ Ⓑ Ⓒ Ⓓ Ⓔ	43 Ⓐ Ⓑ Ⓒ Ⓓ Ⓔ
14 Ⓐ Ⓑ Ⓒ Ⓓ Ⓔ	44 Ⓐ Ⓑ Ⓒ Ⓓ Ⓔ
15 Ⓐ Ⓑ Ⓒ Ⓓ Ⓔ	45 Ⓐ Ⓑ Ⓒ Ⓓ Ⓔ
16 Ⓐ Ⓑ Ⓒ Ⓓ Ⓔ	46 Ⓐ Ⓑ Ⓒ Ⓓ Ⓔ
17 Ⓐ Ⓑ Ⓒ Ⓓ Ⓔ	47 Ⓐ Ⓑ Ⓒ Ⓓ Ⓔ
18 Ⓐ Ⓑ Ⓒ Ⓓ Ⓔ	48 Ⓐ Ⓑ Ⓒ Ⓓ Ⓔ
19 Ⓐ Ⓑ Ⓒ Ⓓ Ⓔ	49 Ⓐ Ⓑ Ⓒ Ⓓ Ⓔ
20 Ⓐ Ⓑ Ⓒ Ⓓ Ⓔ	50 Ⓐ Ⓑ Ⓒ Ⓓ Ⓔ
21 Ⓐ Ⓑ Ⓒ Ⓓ Ⓔ	51 Ⓐ Ⓑ Ⓒ Ⓓ Ⓔ
22 Ⓐ Ⓑ Ⓒ Ⓓ Ⓔ	52 Ⓐ Ⓑ Ⓒ Ⓓ Ⓔ
23 Ⓐ Ⓑ Ⓒ Ⓓ Ⓔ	53 Ⓐ Ⓑ Ⓒ Ⓓ Ⓔ
24 Ⓐ Ⓑ Ⓒ Ⓓ Ⓔ	54 Ⓐ Ⓑ Ⓒ Ⓓ Ⓔ
25 Ⓐ Ⓑ Ⓒ Ⓓ Ⓔ	55 Ⓐ Ⓑ Ⓒ Ⓓ Ⓔ
26 Ⓐ Ⓑ Ⓒ Ⓓ Ⓔ	56 Ⓐ Ⓑ Ⓒ Ⓓ Ⓔ
27 Ⓐ Ⓑ Ⓒ Ⓓ Ⓔ	57 Ⓐ Ⓑ Ⓒ Ⓓ Ⓔ
28 Ⓐ Ⓑ Ⓒ Ⓓ Ⓔ	58 Ⓐ Ⓑ Ⓒ Ⓓ Ⓔ
29 Ⓐ Ⓑ Ⓒ Ⓓ Ⓔ	59 Ⓐ Ⓑ Ⓒ Ⓓ Ⓔ
30 Ⓐ Ⓑ Ⓒ Ⓓ Ⓔ	60 Ⓐ Ⓑ Ⓒ Ⓓ Ⓔ

Test 2 - Checking Information	
1 Ⓐ Ⓑ Ⓒ Ⓓ Ⓔ	31 Ⓐ Ⓑ Ⓒ Ⓓ Ⓔ
2 Ⓐ Ⓑ Ⓒ Ⓓ Ⓔ	32 Ⓐ Ⓑ Ⓒ Ⓓ Ⓔ
3 Ⓐ Ⓑ Ⓒ Ⓓ Ⓔ	33 Ⓐ Ⓑ Ⓒ Ⓓ Ⓔ
4 Ⓐ Ⓑ Ⓒ Ⓓ Ⓔ	34 Ⓐ Ⓑ Ⓒ Ⓓ Ⓔ
5 Ⓐ Ⓑ Ⓒ Ⓓ Ⓔ	35 Ⓐ Ⓑ Ⓒ Ⓓ Ⓔ
6 Ⓐ Ⓑ Ⓒ Ⓓ Ⓔ	36 Ⓐ Ⓑ Ⓒ Ⓓ Ⓔ
7 Ⓐ Ⓑ Ⓒ Ⓓ Ⓔ	37 Ⓐ Ⓑ Ⓒ Ⓓ Ⓔ
8 Ⓐ Ⓑ Ⓒ Ⓓ Ⓔ	38 Ⓐ Ⓑ Ⓒ Ⓓ Ⓔ
9 Ⓐ Ⓑ Ⓒ Ⓓ Ⓔ	39 Ⓐ Ⓑ Ⓒ Ⓓ Ⓔ
10 Ⓐ Ⓑ Ⓒ Ⓓ Ⓔ	40 Ⓐ Ⓑ Ⓒ Ⓓ Ⓔ
11 Ⓐ Ⓑ Ⓒ Ⓓ Ⓔ	41 Ⓐ Ⓑ Ⓒ Ⓓ Ⓔ
12 Ⓐ Ⓑ Ⓒ Ⓓ Ⓔ	42 Ⓐ Ⓑ Ⓒ Ⓓ Ⓔ
13 Ⓐ Ⓑ Ⓒ Ⓓ Ⓔ	43 Ⓐ Ⓑ Ⓒ Ⓓ Ⓔ
14 Ⓐ Ⓑ Ⓒ Ⓓ Ⓔ	44 Ⓐ Ⓑ Ⓒ Ⓓ Ⓔ
15 Ⓐ Ⓑ Ⓒ Ⓓ Ⓔ	45 Ⓐ Ⓑ Ⓒ Ⓓ Ⓔ
16 Ⓐ Ⓑ Ⓒ Ⓓ Ⓔ	46 Ⓐ Ⓑ Ⓒ Ⓓ Ⓔ
17 Ⓐ Ⓑ Ⓒ Ⓓ Ⓔ	47 Ⓐ Ⓑ Ⓒ Ⓓ Ⓔ
18 Ⓐ Ⓑ Ⓒ Ⓓ Ⓔ	48 Ⓐ Ⓑ Ⓒ Ⓓ Ⓔ
19 Ⓐ Ⓑ Ⓒ Ⓓ Ⓔ	49 Ⓐ Ⓑ Ⓒ Ⓓ Ⓔ
20 Ⓐ Ⓑ Ⓒ Ⓓ Ⓔ	50 Ⓐ Ⓑ Ⓒ Ⓓ Ⓔ
21 Ⓐ Ⓑ Ⓒ Ⓓ Ⓔ	
22 Ⓐ Ⓑ Ⓒ Ⓓ Ⓔ	
23 Ⓐ Ⓑ Ⓒ Ⓓ Ⓔ	
24 Ⓐ Ⓑ Ⓒ Ⓓ Ⓔ	
25 Ⓐ Ⓑ Ⓒ Ⓓ Ⓔ	
26 Ⓐ Ⓑ Ⓒ Ⓓ Ⓔ	
27 Ⓐ Ⓑ Ⓒ Ⓓ Ⓔ	
28 Ⓐ Ⓑ Ⓒ Ⓓ Ⓔ	
29 Ⓐ Ⓑ Ⓒ Ⓓ Ⓔ	**PLEASE TURN OVER**
30 Ⓐ Ⓑ Ⓒ Ⓓ Ⓔ	

Test 3 - Working with Numbers

1 (A)(B)(C)(D)(E)	26 (A)(B)(C)(D)(E)
2 (A)(B)(C)(D)(E)	27 (A)(B)(C)(D)(E)
3 (A)(B)(C)(D)(E)	28 (A)(B)(C)(D)(E)
4 (A)(B)(C)(D)(E)	29 (A)(B)(C)(D)(E)
5 (A)(B)(C)(D)(E)	30 (A)(B)(C)(D)(E)
6 (A)(B)(C)(D)(E)	31 (A)(B)(C)(D)(E)
7 (A)(B)(C)(D)(E)	32 (A)(B)(C)(D)(E)
8 (A)(B)(C)(D)(E)	33 (A)(B)(C)(D)(E)
9 (A)(B)(C)(D)(E)	34 (A)(B)(C)(D)(E)
10 (A)(B)(C)(D)(E)	35 (A)(B)(C)(D)(E)
11 (A)(B)(C)(D)(E)	36 (A)(B)(C)(D)(E)
12 (A)(B)(C)(D)(E)	37 (A)(B)(C)(D)(E)
13 (A)(B)(C)(D)(E)	38 (A)(B)(C)(D)(E)
14 (A)(B)(C)(D)(E)	39 (A)(B)(C)(D)(E)
15 (A)(B)(C)(D)(E)	40 (A)(B)(C)(D)(E)
16 (A)(B)(C)(D)(E)	41 (A)(B)(C)(D)(E)
17 (A)(B)(C)(D)(E)	42 (A)(B)(C)(D)(E)
18 (A)(B)(C)(D)(E)	43 (A)(B)(C)(D)(E)
19 (A)(B)(C)(D)(E)	44 (A)(B)(C)(D)(E)
20 (A)(B)(C)(D)(E)	45 (A)(B)(C)(D)(E)
21 (A)(B)(C)(D)(E)	46 (A)(B)(C)(D)(E)
22 (A)(B)(C)(D)(E)	47 (A)(B)(C)(D)(E)
23 (A)(B)(C)(D)(E)	48 (A)(B)(C)(D)(E)
24 (A)(B)(C)(D)(E)	49 (A)(B)(C)(D)(E)
25 (A)(B)(C)(D)(E)	50 (A)(B)(C)(D)(E)

Test 4 - Verbal Reasoning

1 (A)(B)(C)(D)(E)	26 (A)(B)(C)(D)(E)
2 (A)(B)(C)(D)(E)	27 (A)(B)(C)(D)(E)
3 (A)(B)(C)(D)(E)	28 (A)(B)(C)(D)(E)
4 (A)(B)(C)(D)(E)	29 (A)(B)(C)(D)(E)
5 (A)(B)(C)(D)(E)	30 (A)(B)(C)(D)(E)
6 (A)(B)(C)(D)(E)	31 (A)(B)(C)(D)(E)
7 (A)(B)(C)(D)(E)	32 (A)(B)(C)(D)(E)
8 (A)(B)(C)(D)(E)	33 (A)(B)(C)(D)(E)
9 (A)(B)(C)(D)(E)	34 (A)(B)(C)(D)(E)
10 (A)(B)(C)(D)(E)	35 (A)(B)(C)(D)(E)
11 (A)(B)(C)(D)(E)	36 (A)(B)(C)(D)(E)
12 (A)(B)(C)(D)(E)	37 (A)(B)(C)(D)(E)
13 (A)(B)(C)(D)(E)	38 (A)(B)(C)(D)(E)
14 (A)(B)(C)(D)(E)	39 (A)(B)(C)(D)(E)
15 (A)(B)(C)(D)(E)	40 (A)(B)(C)(D)(E)
16 (A)(B)(C)(D)(E)	41 (A)(B)(C)(D)(E)
17 (A)(B)(C)(D)(E)	42 (A)(B)(C)(D)(E)
18 (A)(B)(C)(D)(E)	43 (A)(B)(C)(D)(E)
19 (A)(B)(C)(D)(E)	44 (A)(B)(C)(D)(E)
20 (A)(B)(C)(D)(E)	45 (A)(B)(C)(D)(E)
21 (A)(B)(C)(D)(E)	46 (A)(B)(C)(D)(E)
22 (A)(B)(C)(D)(E)	47 (A)(B)(C)(D)(E)
23 (A)(B)(C)(D)(E)	48 (A)(B)(C)(D)(E)
24 (A)(B)(C)(D)(E)	49 (A)(B)(C)(D)(E)
25 (A)(B)(C)(D)(E)	50 (A)(B)(C)(D)(E)

Test 5 - Observation

1 (A)(B)(C)	8 (A)(B)(C)
2 (A)(B)(C)	9 (A)(B)(C)
3 (A)(B)(C)	10 (A)(B)(C)
4 (A)(B)(C)	11 (A)(B)(C)
5 (A)(B)(C)	12 (A)(B)(C)
6 (A)(B)(C)	13 (A)(B)(C)
7 (A)(B)(C)	14 (A)(B)(C)

Test1 – Verbal Usage

In the following sentences, two words need to be inserted to make the sentence read sensibly. Choose the correct pair of words and mark A, B, C, D or E on your answer sheet by completely filling in the circle.

---

1. Thirteen people were_____ for breaching the _____ .

A	B	C	D	E
arrested	arrested	arested	arested	none of these
piece	peace	piece	peace	

---

2. Fred _____ money from the prepayment gas _____ at his home.

A	B	C	D	E
steels	steals	steals	steels	none of these
meter	metre	meter	metre	

---

3. The _____ for the prosecution proved _____ .

A	B	C	D	E
witness	wittness	witness	wittness	none of these
unreliable	unrelyable	unnreliable	unrelyable	

---

4. A police car arrived at the _____ almost _____ .

A	B	C	D	E
seen	scene	seen	scene	none of these
imediatly	immediatly	immediatly	immediately	

---

5. Highjacking is the _____ use of force or threats to _____ an aircraft.

A	B	C	D	E
unlawful	unlawful	unlawfull	unlawfull	none of these
seize	sieze	seize	sieze	

---

6. _____ action may be called for in an _____ .

A	B	C	D	E
Couragous	Courageous	Couragous	Courageous	none of these
emergency	emergency	emergancy	emergancy	

7. The _____ was suspected of _____ under the influence of drink.

A	B	C	D	E
defendant	defendant	defendent	defendent	none of these
driving	driveing	driving	driveing	

8. One man _____ innocent but the others _____ guilty.

A	B	C	D	E
pleaded	pleaded	pleeded	pleeded	none of these
were	was	were	was	

9. A _____ goods vehicle is a goods vehicle which has been brought into Great _____ .

A	B	C	D	E
forign	foreign	foriegn	foreign	none of these
britain	Britan	Britain	Britain	

10. Crossing double white lines to overtake a _____ vehicle is not _____ .

A	B	C	D	E
stationery	stationary	stationery	stationary	none of these
ilegal	illegal	ilegal	illegall	

11. Crossing double white lines to overtake moving _____ is an _____ .

A	B	C	D	E
veicles	vehicles	vehicles	veicles	none of these
ofence	offence	offense	ofense	

12.   The policeman was not entirely _____ with the_____
for trespass.

A	B	C	D	E
satisfyed	satisfyed	satisfied	satisfied	none of these
reeson	reason	reason	reeson	

---

13.   _____ sense is important in car _____ .

A	B	C	D	E
Aceleration	Aceleration	Acelleration	Aceleration	none of these
control	controle	control	controle	

---

14.   You need plenty of _____ for a _____ test.

A	B	C	D	E
practise	practise	practice	practise	none of these
successful	successfull	successful	sucessful	

---

15.   Some _____ premises seem to cater _____ for the criminal element.

A	B	C	D	E
licensed	licenced	licensed	licenced	none of these
exclusivly	exclusivley	exclusively	exclusivley	

---

16.   A man of _____ build entered the building via a side _____ .

A	B	C	D	E
muscular	musculer	muscular	musculer	none of these
entrance	enterence	enterance	entrence	

---

17.   Of the crimes _____ , the first had been the _____ .

A	B	C	D	E
comited	comited	committed	comitted	none of these
worse	worser	worst	worsest	

18. He _____ the offence knowing _____ was useless.

A	B	C	D	E
addmitted	admitted	admitted	addmitted	none of these
denyal	denial	denyial	denial	

---

19. The man was _____ in an attempt to _____ the police.

A	B	C	D	E
lieing	lieing	lying	lying	none of these
deceave	deceive	decieve	deceive	

---

20. There was insufficient _____ to instigate _____ .

A	B	C	D	E
evidance	evidance	evidence	evidence	none of these
procedings	proceedings	proseedings	proceedings	

---

21. Aircraft should not be flown so as to cause _____ danger to any person or _____ .

A	B	C	D	E
unecesary	unnecessary	unnecesary	unecesery	none of these
property	property	propety	proparty	

---

22. At _____ miles per hour, the car crossed the _____ reservation.

A	B	C	D	E
eigthy	eighty	eighty	eighty	none of these
central	central	centeral	centrel	

---

23. Noise pollution is a _____ but not a _____ offence.

A	B	C	D	E
nuisance	nuisanse	newsance	newsanse	none of these
chargeable	chargable	chargeable	chargable	

24. If he had driven more _____ an _____ could have been avoided.

A	B	C	D	E
careful	carefull	carefuly	carefully	none of these
acident	acident	accident	accident	

25. _____ of one of the _____ were informed.

A	B	C	D	E
Reletives	Relitives	Relatives	Relertives	none of these
deseased	diceased	deceased	diseased	

26. Giving false _____ is a _____ of police time.

A	B	C	D	E
testamony	testimony	testimony	testamony	none of these
waist	waste	waist	waste	

27. Detective's work is based on _____ inquiry, patient observation and good _____ .

A	B	C	D	E
persistant	persistant	pursistant	pursistent	none of these
information	imformation	information	imformation	

28. A thorough _____ had failed to reveal who was responsible for the _____ .

A	B	C	D	E
investigation	investagation	investigation	investegation	none of these
robbory	robery	roberry	robbory	

29. The police _____ the attack was of a _____ nature.

A	B	C	D	E
beleaved	beleived	believed	believed	none of these
racist	rasist	rasist	racist	

30. The judge _____ the guilty man serve the full _____ .

A	B	C	D	E
recomended	recommended	recommended	recomended	none of these
sentence	sentence	sentance	sentance	

31. An ambulance team tried _____ to _____ the man.

A	B	C	D	E
desprately	desprately	desperately	desperately	none of these
resusitate	resussitate	resuscitate	resusitate	

32. Sarah was found _____ of _____ manslaughter.

A	B	C	D	E
guilty	guillty	guillty	guilty	none of these
involuntary	involluntary	involuntary	involuntarry	

33. The _____ driver _____ the car with ease.

A	B	C	D	E
skillful	skilful	skillfull	skilfull	none of these
manouvred	manoeuvred	manouvred	manouevred	

34. Williamson was charged with resisiting _____ and causing _____ bodily harm.

A	B	C	D	E
arrest	arrest	arest	arest	none of these
grevious	grievious	grevious	grievious	

35. Both men _____ nervous during _____ interrogation.

A	B	C	D	E
apeared	apeared	appeared	appeared	none of these
their	there	there	their	

36. Jim was _____ by a witness a being _____ for a burglary at a shop.

A	B	C	D	E
identifyed responsible	identifyed responsible	identified responsible	identified responsable	none of these

37. The car passed _____ MOT on _____ .

A	B	C	D	E
it's Wendsday	its Wendsday	it's Wednesday	its Wednesday	none of these

38. All the _____ was bagged and _____ after fingerprinting.

A	B	C	D	E
jewelry labled	jewellery labelled	jewelry labelled	jewellery labled	none of these

39. The case against the _____ was based _____ on circumstantial evidence.

A	B	C	D	E
accused entirely	acused entirely	accused entirley	acused entireley	none of these

40. Patience and _____ are essential in a _____ situation.

A	B	C	D	E
dissiplin seige	disciplin siege	discipline siege	disipline seige	none of these

41. He was found in _____ of _____ property.

A	B	C	D	E
posesion stollen	possesion stollen	posession stolen	possession stolen	none of these

42. Further _____ with Scotland Yard would be _____ .

A	B	C	D	E
liason	liason	liason	liaison	none of these
necessary	necessary	necessary	necesary	

---

43. The driver's _____ of First Aid saved the _____ man's life.

A	B	C	D	E
knowledge	knoledge	knowlidge	knolege	none of these
injured	injured	injurred	injurred	

---

44. All leave was _____ due to the _____ overload.

A	B	C	D	E
cancelled	canceled	cancelled	canceled	none of these
aditional	additional	additional	aditional	

---

45. Williams was charged with _____ with a deadly _____ .

A	B	C	D	E
assalt	assalt	assault	assault	none of these
wepon	weapon	wepon	weapon	

---

46. Firemen broke into the _____ to _____ the family.

A	B	C	D	E
residense	residence	residance	residence	none of these
rescew	rescue	rescue	rescuew	

---

47. The suspect's _____ was under constant _____ .

A	B	C	D	E
addres	adress	adress	addres	none of these
surveilance	surveilance	surveillance	surveillance	

---

48. His letter ended Yours _____ instead of Yours _____.

A	B	C	D	E
faithfully	faithfuly	faithfully	faithfuly	none of these
sincerely	sincerely	sincerelly	sincerley	

49. _____ of the prisoners seemed _____.

A	B	C	D	E
Neither	Neither	Niether	Niether	none of these
nervus	nerves	nervous	nervous	

50. The _____ gave the man a _____.

A	B	C	D	E
sergant	sargant	sergeant	sargeant	none of these
sigarette	cigarete	cigarette	cigarette	

51. If the evidence was _____ then the prosecution would be _____.

A	B	C	D	E
corroborated	coroberated	coroborated	coroborated	none of these
successful	succsessfull	successful	successfull	

52. Special constables with less than two year's service are not _____ to carry out patrols unless_____.

A	B	C	D	E
alloud	allowed	alloud	allowed	none of these
accompanied	accompanied	acompanied	acompanied	

53. A _____ enpowers police to enter premises using force if _____.

A	B	C	D	E
warrant	warant	warant	warrant	none of these
necessary	necessary	necesary	necessery	

54. The car was travelling _____ fast _____ stop in time.

A	B	C	D	E
to	too	to	too	none of these
to	too	too	to	

---

55. It was the _____ evidence that _____ the man.

A	B	C	D	E
neihgbour's	neihbours	neighbours	neihbours	none of these
condemned	condemed	condemned	condemed	

---

56. A _____ of the USA has the right to take the life of another in _____ of himself, his family or property.

A	B	C	D	E
cityzen	cityzan	citizan	citizen	none of these
defense	defense	defence	defence	

---

57. _____ expenditure on police vehicles runs into tens of _____ of pounds .

A	B	C	D	E
Anual	Annuall	Annual	Annuall	none of these
Milions	millions	millions	milions	

---

58. It was thought that the _____ was still in the _____.

A	B	C	D	E
supplyer	supplier	supplyer	supplier	none of these
locality	locality	locallity	locallity	

---

59. His _____ left him _____ .

A	B	C	D	E
assailant	assailent	assallent	assailant	none of these
bleading	bleeding	bleading	bleeding	

---

60.   Detectives entered the house _____ so as not to _____ the suspects.

A	B	C	D	E
disscretly	disscretely	discreetly	discreetly	none of these
allert	allert	alert	allert	

Test 2 – Checking Information

In the two lists below, check to see whether the information in List 1 has been correctly transferred to List 2. Fill in the circles on your answer sheet corresponding with the errors in the columns (A,B,C and D). If there are there are no errors, fill in circle E. There may be more than one error in a line.

	List 1				List 2			
	A	**B**	**C**	**D**	**A**	**B**	**C**	**D**
	Date	Name	Time	Ref No.	Date	Name	Time	Ref No.
1.	24.2	Carver	09.21	1016	Feb 28	CARVER	09.21	1016
2.	5.11	Scott	23.57	7020	Nov 5	SCOTT	22.57	7022
3.	5.10	Rodgers	17.32	3735	May 10	ROGERS	17.32	3738
4.	8.7	Newman	07.05	2256	Aug 8	NEWMAN	07.08	2256
5.	23.4	MacFarlan	14.56	1676	Apr 23	McFARLAN	14.56	1676
6.	10.12	Hughes	20.50	4143	Dec 10	HUGHES	20.50	4144
7.	15.3	Tyler	10.16	1548	Sept 3	TYRER	10.16	1548
8.	9.1	Kelly	02.32	9655	Jan 4	KELLY	02.23	9565
9.	1.6	Parry	18.24	906	June 1	PARRY	16.24	609
10.	6.5	Fox	11.30	4568	May 6	FOX	11.30	4568
11.	5. 11	Dyer	05.34	1223	Nov 11	DIER	05.34	1232
12.	3.2	Marshal	21.43	3619	July 6	MARSHALL	21.43	3619
13.	15.10	Cooper	16.27	5321	Oct 14	COOPER	16.27	5321
14.	7.8	Sampson	23.17	7147	Aug 7	SAMSON	23.17	7147
15.	2.3	Holmes	08.35	8415	March 2	HOMES	05.35	8145
16.	8.9	Ishmael	13.25	1046	Sept 9	ISHMAEL	13.35	1046
17.	14.6	Canning	15.57	4389	June 14	CANNING	15.57	4389
18.	21.12	Almand	04.48	6674	Dec 22	ALMOND	04.48	6964
19.	1.1	Lindsay	15.30	2619	April 1	LINDSEY	17.30	2619
20.	12.8	Urmston	20.12	3347	Aug 12	URMSTON	20.12	3347
21.	20.2	Ansari	14.45	2453	Jan 20	ANSARI	14.55	2458
22.	6.7	Daniels	06.30	8757	July 6	DANIELS	06.30	8757
23.	15.10	Baylis	02.31	6389	Aug 15	BAYLISS	02.13	6389
24.	9.7	Vaughan	23.23	7492	Aug 8	VAUGHN	22.23	9578
25.	17.5	Howells	11.56	9875	May 17	HOWELLS	11.56	9875
26.	12.10	Bardsley	14.50	8583	Oct 12	BARDSEY	14.50	8583
27.	12. 23	Lovell	06.15	2839	Dec 23	LOVELL	09.15	2839
28.	4.6	Grosvenor	13.35	3495	June 4	GROVENOR	3.35	3465
29.	8.5	Gallacher	23.08	7842	May 5	GALLAGER	23.08	7842
30.	29.9	Dewhurst	08.12	1028	Sept 29	DEWHURST	08.40	1038

Test 2 -Continued

The table below contains information about stolen goods. This information has been <u>transferred on to the computer</u> and errors have been made. Fill in the circles on the answer sheet (A, B, C, D) corresponding with the errors in the computer columns. If there are no errors fill in circle E.

31. Owner: Stephens
    Bike description:
    Mr Mrs Miss Ms
    Boys BMX Stunt
    Date: 26 January
    Serial no: TX258221

32. Owner:Crossley
    Bike description:
    Mr Mrs Miss **Ms**
    Townsend Tourer
    Date: 6 July
    Serial no: CL714976

33. Owner: Rowcott
    Bike description:
    Mr Mrs Miss Ms
    Claud Butler Mens
    Date: 21 November
    Serial no: WR874520

34. Owner: McKay
    Bike description:
    Mr Mrs **Miss** Ms
    Saracen Off-Road
    Date: 30 September
    Serial no: MNX48292

35. Owner: Walla
    Bike description:
    Mr Mrs Miss Ms
    Raleigh Mountain
    Date: 3 February
    Serial no: 3287428

36. Owner: Gunther
    Bike description:
    Mr **Mrs** Miss Ms
    Falcon Ladies 18-speed
    Date: 9 May
    Serial no: 8471879

37. Owner: Elliot
    Bike description:
    Mr Mrs Miss Ms
    Gents Triumph Road
    Date: 11 October
    Serial no: 1972972

38. Owner: Bishop
    Bike description:
    Mr Mrs **Miss** Ms
    Ladies Peugeot Racing
    Date: 16 July
    Serial: 343327TY

39. Owner: Stone
    Bike description:
    Mr **Mrs** Miss Ms
    Muddy Fox All Terrain
    Date: 3 April
    Serial no: PY329871

40. Owner: Prescott
    Bike description:
    Mr Mrs Miss **Ms**
    Dawes Mountain Bike
    Date: 24 August
    Serial no: 54335697

41. Owner: Pritchard
    Watch description:
    Mr Mrs Miss Ms
    Alfred Dunhill Watch
    Date: 10 December
    White Face

42. Owner: Bushell
    Watch description:
    Mr Mrs Miss Ms
    Mens Rolex Watch
    Date: 20 March
    Sea Dweller

43. Owner: Quigley
    Jewellery description:
    Mr **Mrs** Miss Ms
    Gold Bracelet
    Date: 5 November
    9ct 110g

44. Owner: Menzies
    Jewellery description:
    Mr Mrs **Miss** Ms
    Diamond Solitaire
    Date: 2 January
    0.65 ct

45. Owner: Maddocks
    Camera description:
    Mr Mrs Miss **Ms**
    Canon EOS1000
    Date: 14 June
    Serial no: 7439847

46. Owner: Mugabi
    Camera description:
    Mr Mrs Miss Ms
    Nikon F25B body
    Date: 12 October
    Serial no: 917243221

47. Owner: Godber
    Car stereo:
    Mr **Mrs** Miss Ms
    Kenwood KDC
    Date: 24 May
    Model no: 4060RA

48. Owner: Aziz
    Car stereo:
    Mr Mrs Miss **Ms**
    Sony CDX
    Date: 30 September
    Model no: 4180R

49. Owner: Bishop
    Phone description:
    Mr Mrs Miss Ms
    Ericsson PH388
    Date: 22 July
    Serial no:38749TE

50. Owner: Johnston
    Phone description:
    Mr **Mrs** Miss Ms
    Nokia nk402
    Date: 29 September
    Serial no: 37692DS

COMPUTER

	A Date	B Description	C Number	D Owner
31.	26/10	BMX Stunt Bike	TX258212	Mr Stevens
32.	7/6	Townsend Tourer	CL714976	Ms Crossley
33.	21/11	Claude Butler Mens	WR8755420	Mr Rowcott
34.	30/9	Saracen Off-Road	MNX48292	Miss Mckay
35.	3/2	Raleigh Mountain	3287428	Mr Walla
36.	9/5	Falcon Ladies 15-speed	8471879	Mrs Gunther
37.	11/10	Gents Triumph Road	1972972	Mr Elliott
38.	16/7	Ladies Peugot Racing	343327TY	Miss Bishop
39.	4/3	Muddy Fox All Terrain	329871PY	Mrs Stone
40.	24/9	Daws Mountain Bike	54335697	Ms Prescot
41.	10/12	Alfred Dunhill Watch	White Face	Mrs Pritchard
42.	20/3	Mens Rolex Watch	Sea Dweller	Mr Bushell
43.	5/10	Gold Bracelet	19ct 10g	Ms Quigley
44.	1/2	Diamond Solitaire	0.55ct	Miss Mensies
45.	14/6	Canon EOS1000	7439857	Ms Maddocks
46.	2/10	Nikon F2SB body	917243221	Mr Mugaby
47.	24/6	Kenwood KDC	4060HA	Mrs Godber
48.	30/9	Sony CD	4810R	Ms Aziz
49.	22/7	Ericsson PH388	38749TE	Mr Bishop
50.	29/8	Nokia kn402	37962DS	Mrs Johnson

This page has been deliberately left blank.

Test 3 – Working with Numbers (to be done without using a calculator)

Choose the correct answer and mark A, B, C, D or E on your answer sheet by completely filling in the circle.

1. This month a man's pay is £360 basic plus £95 overtime. What is his total pay?

A	B	C	D	E
£450	£455	£460	£465	£470

2. A factory has 414 employees. If 25 are absent, how many are present?

A	B	C	D	E
379	380	389	390	398

3. Time in New York is 5 hours behind Greenwhich Mean Time. If it is 1730 hours GMT, what time is it in New York?.

A	B	C	D	E
2230	1030	1230	0730	1730

4. How long does it take a bus travelling at an average speed of 44 mph to cover 132 miles?.

A	B	C	D	E
1 hr	2 hrs	2.5hrs	3 hrs	3.5 hrs

5. What is the floor area in square feet of a room 12' long x 11' wide?

A	B	C	D	E
144	132	121	110	108

6. If the HP payments on a HiFi system are £20 per month, how much will be paid at the end of 3 years?

A	B	C	D	E
£240	£360	£480	£720	£1440

7. A lottery syndicate wins £10000. If there are 25 people in the syndicate, how much money will each person receive?

A	B	C	D	E
£1000	£500	£400	£250	£200

8. A quarter pound of minced beef is needed to make one beefburger. How many beefburgers can be made from 6 pounds of beef?

A	B	C	D	E
25	24	23	22	20

9. A tyre can be inflated to 30 psi ± 20%. What is the maximum pressure the tyre can be inflated to?

A	B	C	D	E
30 psi	32 psi	34 psi	36 psi	38 psi

10. On a map of scale 1 to 25000 the distance between two cities is represented by a line 10 cm long. What is the actual distance in km?

A	B	C	D	E
2.5 km	5 km	10 km	15 km	20 km

11. A girl sets off by bicycle on a journey of 40 km . If she arrives at her destination 2.5 hours later, what was her average speed (km per hour).

A	B	C	D	E
10	16	20	25	40

12. How many grams are there in 1.5 kg?

A	B	C	D	E
15	150	1500	15000	150000

13. In a group of 50 applicants 80% are male. How many females are there?

A	B	C	D	E
10	20	30	40	50

14. Three men left the Forces aged 25, 30 and 35. What was the average leaving age?

A	B	C	D	E
25	27	29	30	33

15. A discount of 10% is offered on an article priced £8.90. How much will the purchaser pay?

A	B	C	D	E
£7.90	£7.91	£8.00	£8.01	£8.09

16. Twenty packets of drugs each contain 50 grams each. What is the total weight of drugs in kilograms?

A	B	C	D	E
0.5	1.0	10	50	100

17. A car uses 5 litres of petrol for every 50 km. How far can it travel on 10 litres of fuel?

A	B	C	D	E
5 km	10 km	50 km	100 km	500 km

18. The cost of a hired minibus shared equally between 12 people is £4.50. What is the cost of hiring the minibus?

A	B	C	D	E
£48	£54	£60	£66	£72

19. The cost of 500 g of ham at £2.40 per kg is:

A	B	C	D	E
12p	£24p	£1.20	£2.40	£12.00

20. In a parliamentary constituency 7500 out of 10000 people voted. What percentage of the people did not vote?

A	B	C	D	E
5%	10%	15%	20%	25%

21. How many pieces of string 20 cm long can be cut from a 10 m length?

A	B	C	D	E
0	5	50	500	5000

22. A garage sells a car and makes a profit of 25% on the cost price. If the cost price is £4000 what is the selling price?

A	B	C	D	E
£4000	£5000	£6000	£7000	£8000

23. 5000 mm expressed in metres is:

A	B	C	D	E
0.05 m	0.5 m	5 m	50 m	500 m

24. A purse was handed in with two one pound coins, five twenty pence pieces and five two pence coins. How much does it contain.

A	B	C	D	E
£2.10	£2.60	£3.00	£3.10	£3.60

25. What percentage of 80 is 16?

A	B	C	D	E
10%	20%	25%	40%	45%

26. A kettle boils 3 pints of water in 3 minutes. How long will it take to boil half a pint of water?

A	B	C	D	E
1.5 minutes	1 minute	30 seconds	9 seconds	3 seconds

27. The repair bill on a car came to £500. If the insurance company paid 90 % of this, how much did they pay?

A	B	C	D	E
£90	£180	£410	£430	£450

28. A tea urn has a capacity of 20 litres. How many cups of tea will it make if the cups hold 250 ml each?

A	B	C	D	E
10	25	40	80	100

29. The normal price of a certain pair of trousers is £28. This is reduced by 25% in a sale. What is the sale price of the trousers?

A	B	C	D	E
£20	£21	£22	£23	£24

30. A builder has 50000 bricks; a further 5500 are ordered and 6000 are used to build a wall. How many are left?

A	B	C	D	E
49500	49000	48500	48000	47500

31. If £10 buys $15, how many dollars would you receive for £50?

A	B	C	D	E
$50	$60	$65	$70	$75

32. A man saves 4% of his annual income of £18 000. How much does he save?

A	B	C	D	E
£18	£72	£400	£650	£720

---

33. A meal for 10 people costs £200 plus tax added at a rate of 17.5%. How much is the tax?

A	B	C	D	E
£10	£17	£20	£35	£75

---

34. A typist can type 50 words per minute? How long will it take to type a 3000 word report?

A	B	C	D	E
6 minutes	1 hour	2 hours	3 hours	6 hours

---

35. £10 is shared between two people in the ratio of 2:3. How much is the smaller share?

A	B	C	D	E
£6	£5	£4	£3	£2

---

36. A bank pays 6.5% interest per annum on a deposit account? By how much will £200 have grown in 12 months?

A	B	C	D	E
£6.50	£12	£13	£24	£65

---

37. A tank measuring 3m x 3m x 3m is one third full of water. What is the volume of water in m^3 ?

A	B	C	D	E
9	6	3	2	1

---

38.   A lorry driver travels 100 miles at an average speed of 50 mph. If he has a half hour lunch break, how long does the journey take?

A	B	C	D	E
4.5 hours	4 hours	3.5 hours	3 hours	2.5 hours

---

39.   A train departs at 0730 hrs and arrives at its destination at 1330 hrs. How long does the journey take?

A	B	C	D	E
6 hours	5 hours	4 hours	3 hours	2 hours

---

40.   A man earning £280 per week is awarded a 10% pay rise. What will be his new weekly wage?

A	B	C	D	E
£290	£298	£300	£308	£318

---

41.   A vending machine contains 12 fifty pence and 18 ten pence coins. How much is this altogether?

A	B	C	D	E
£7.80	£78	£13.80	£6	£28

---

42.   A film lasted 120 minutes. The last show begins at 8.15 p.m. At what time will it finish?

A	B	C	D	E
10.00hrs	10.15hrs	20.15hrs	22.00hrs	22.15hrs

---

43.   What is the perimeter of a rectangular bowling green measuring 40 metres long and 35 metres wide in metres?

A	B	C	D	E
35	40	70	150	1400

44. Out of a sample of 1000 people, 82% watched the television on a Saturday night. How many did not watch television that night?

A	B	C	D	E
0	18	82	180	1000

45. Three people aged 17, 20 and 23 sit a test. What is the average age?

A	B	C	D	E
21	20	19	18	17

46. Stephen exchanged £400 for German Marks at an exchange rate of £1 = 2.50 DM. How many Marks did she receive?

A	B	C	D	E
500	750	800	1000	2000

47. Mr Clarke drove for one and a half hours at an average speed of 50 mph. How far did he travel?

A	B	C	D	E
75 miles	85 miles	90 miles	95 miles	100 miles

48. Aziz's electricity bill comprises 1000 units at 7p per unit plus a standing charge of £15.00. How much does he have to pay?

A	B	C	D	E
£20	£21	£22	£23	£24

49. A washing machine was paid for with a deposit £100 and 10 Instalments of £25. What was the total cost?

A	B	C	D	E
£400	£350	£300	£250	£125

50. What is the missing number in the sequence: 1.5, ---, 2.0, 2.25 2.5?

A	B	C	D	E
1.0	1.25	1.5	1.75	2.0

This page has been deliberately left blank

This page has been deliberately left blank

Test 4- Verbal Reasoning

Read the information in the box, then answer the statements. Mark A on the answer sheet if the statement is true; mark B on the answer sheet if the statement is false; mark C on the answer sheet if it is impossible to say either way.

An officer from the Antiques Squad spotted some familiar looking artefacts in the window of a local antique dealer. An initial investigation revealed the following facts:

- All the familiar artefacts and a few others in the shop, were on a 'stolen list' from a stately home.

- The antique dealer, Don Waine, had no previous convictions for handling stolen goods.

- The man who sold the items to the dealer was described as "upper class".

- Not all of the items stolen from the stately home could be accounted for.

- The insurance company had already paid out in full.

- The stately home was owned by a millionaire.

| A = TRUE | B = FALSE | C = IMPOSSIBLE TO SAY |

1. Don Waine was an antique dealer.

2. All the stolen items could be accounted for.

3. The "upper class" man was definitely the thief.

4. The insurance company stood to benefit from the find.

5. All the artefacts in the shop were on the 'stolen list'.

6. Don Waine could know the identity of the "upper class" man.

7. The owner of the stately home is a wealthy man.

8. Don Waine had committed a criminal offence.

A publican had escorted a heavily built man off the premises. The man had fallen down a flight of stone steps at the entrance to the pub and sustained a broken arm.
The only facts known at this stage are:

- The incident occurred after closing time when everybody else had left the vicinity.

- The heavily built man was the worse for drink.

- An ambulance arrived at the pub at 11.43 pm.

- It was the licensee who telephoned for the ambulance.

- The heavily built man was incoherent.

A = TRUE   B = FALSE   C = IMPOSSIBLE TO SAY

---

9. There were independent witnesses to the incident.

10. The heavily built man was not injured.

11. 'Last orders' were given before the incident took place.

12. The licensee used excessive force to remove the man.

13. The heavily built man was able to make a statement.

14. He could have lost his balance.

15. The ambulance took more than 1 hour to arrive.

16. There are definite grounds to arrest the licensee for grievous bodily harm.

CID had reliable information that Johnson, a local scrap metal dealer was resetting stolen silverware and jewellery. On Saturday, November 8th Johnson and two other men, both male Caucasian, were seen at Johnson's premises.
At this stage the facts are:-

- One of the two other men had a conviction for burglary.

- The third man was not known to the police.

- The known man had been identified as George Lucas.

- Lucas was suspected of stealing property the previous day.

- The police had not had time to obtain a search warrant.

A = TRUE   B = FALSE   C = IMPOSSIBLE TO SAY

17. Lucas was suspected of stealing property on Friday that week.

18. All three men on the premises were known to the police.

19. The dealer was believed to be setting stolen jewellery in different frames.

20. Two of the three men were black.

21. Two of the three men had previous convictions.

22. Lucas could have brought stolen property to the premises.

23. The dealer had stolen property in his possession.

24. There were definite grounds to obtain a search warrant.

The Flying Squad was credited with the arrest of the Great Train Robbers in 1963. Chief superintendent Tommy Butler had identified the principal robbers 24 hours after the crime took place. This success was largely the result of:

- Informants having indicated that a major robbery was being planned, four weeks prior to the crime.

- Tommy Butler having listed the likely leaders.

- Tapping of the suspects telephones.

- Fingerprints found at a farm, used by the villains to launch the robbery.

- Tommy immediately suggesting possible villains to the fingerprint department.

A = TRUE	B = FALSE	C = IMPOSSIBLE TO SAY

25. The Great Train Robbery took place over 40 years ago.

26. No arrests were made within 24 hours.

27. Tommy Butler had some of the suspects on a list.

28. All the villains kept gloves on at the farm.

29. The farm could have been near to the scene of the crime.

30. Matching fingerprints with those of suspects saved time.

31. Tommy Butler had confirmed the identity of the villains four weeks before the train was robbed.

32. Informants knew where the robbery was going to take place.

The police were directed to a road accident which had occurred during the hours of darkness.
The only known facts at this stage are:

- A Ford Fiesta had been driven into the rear of a Montego.

- The driver of the Fiesta was uninjured.

- The Montego was parked on the right side of the road close to a junction.

- Both cars had suffered light damage.

- The Montego was unattended and was not displaying any lights.

- There were no other vehicles involved in the accident.

A = TRUE   B = FALSE   C = IMPOSSIBLE TO SAY

---

33. The Fiesta was badly damaged at the front.

34. The Montego had suffered rear end damage.

35. The Fiesta had been driven without any lights on.

36. A third vehicle was involved.

37. The street lights were not on.

38. Accidents happen all the time so nobody is to blame.

39. The Montego was parked in a one-way street.

40. The driver/owner of the Montego might have committed an offence.

This page has been deliberately left blank

Test 5 – Observation and Memory

Instuctions

Study the picture on page 35 for two minutes then answer the questions on page 39 (circle your answer sheet)

Study the second picture on page 41 for two minutes then answer the questions on page 45.

This page has been deliberately left blank

This page has been deliberately left blank

This page has been deliberately left blank.

This page has been deliberately left blank

1. A man having his passport checked had arrived from:-

A. Canberra
B. Sydney
C. Perth

2. A woman holding skis was saying:

A. I've broken my arm.
B. I've had an accident.
C. My friend's had an accident.

3. An Immigration Officer was asking:-

A. Where are you staying?
B. When are you leaving?
C. How long are you staying?

4. How many people were sitting down?

A. Two
B. One
C. None

5. The luggage trolley had

A. No luggage on it.
B. One bag on it.
C. Two bags on it.

6. The man at the Customs Desk was wearing;-

A. A hat with corks.
B. A beret.
C. A bobble hat.

7. How many people were in uniform?

A. Two people.
B. Three people.
C. Four people.

This page has been deliberately left blank

This page has been deliberately left blank

This page has been deliberately left blank.

This page has been deliberately left blank

8. A man on a telephone was saying he was leaving in:-

A. Ten minutes.
B. Twenty minutes.
C. Thirty minutes.

9. A woman was pointing at an aircraft that:

A. Had taken off.
B. Had landed.
C. Was about to take off.

10. A man waving goodbye was saying:

A. See you next week.
B. See you in two weeks.
C. See you in three weeks.

11. A woman waving goodbye was:

A. Just about to climb the stairs.
B. Half way up the stairs.
C. Near the top of the stairs.

12. The tannoy was indicating that all passengers should go to:

A. Gate 5
B. Gate 7
C. Gate 9

13. The next flight was destined for:-

A. Italy
B. Germany
C. France

14. The flight number was:

A. BA203
B. BA302
C. BA320

This page has been deliberately left blank

ANSWERS

Test 1 - Verbal Usage

#	Ans	#	Ans
1	B	31	C
2	C	32	A
3	A	33	B
4	D	34	E
5	A	35	E
6	B	36	C
7	A	37	D
8	A	38	B
9	D	39	A
10	B	40	C
11	B	41	D
12	C	42	E
13	E	43	A
14	A	44	C
15	C	45	D
16	A	46	B
17	C	47	E
18	B	48	A
19	D	49	E
20	D	50	C
21	B	51	A
22	B	52	B
23	A	53	A
24	D	54	E
25	C	55	E
26	B	56	D
27	A	57	C
28	E	58	B
29	D	59	D
30	B	60	C

Test 2 - Checking Information

#	Ans	#	Ans
1	A	31	B C D
2	C D E	32	A
3	A B E	33	B C
4	A C	34	D
5	B	35	D
6	D	36	B
7	A B	37	A
8	A C	38	B
9	C D E	39	A C
10	E	40	A B C D
11	A B D	41	D
12	A B	42	E
13	A	43	A C D
14	B	44	A C
15	A C D E	45	C
16	A C	46	A C D
17	E	47	A C D
18	A B D E	48	A D
19	A B C	49	E
20	E	50	A B C D
21	A C D E		
22	E		
23	A B C		
24	A B C D		
25	E		
26	B		
27	A C		
28	A		
29	A B		
30	C D		

PLEASE TURN OVER

Test 3 - Working with Numbers

#	A	B	C	D	E		#	A	B	C	D	E
1	A	●	C	D	E		26	A	B	●	D	E
2	A	B	●	D	E		27	A	B	C	D	●
3	A	B	●	D	E		28	A	B	C	●	E
4	A	B	C	●	E		29	A	●	C	D	E
5	A	●	C	D	E		30	●	B	C	D	E
6	A	B	C	●	E		31	A	B	C	D	●
7	A	B	●	D	E		32	A	B	C	D	●
8	A	●	C	D	E		33	A	B	C	●	E
9	A	B	C	●	E		34	A	●	C	D	E
10	●	B	C	D	E		35	A	B	●	D	E
11	A	●	C	D	E		36	A	B	●	D	E
12	A	B	●	D	E		37	●	B	C	D	E
13	●	B	C	D	E		38	A	B	C	D	●
14	A	B	C	●	E		39	●	B	C	D	E
15	A	B	C	●	E		40	A	B	C	●	E
16	A	●	C	D	E		41	●	B	C	D	E
17	A	B	C	●	E		42	A	B	C	D	●
18	A	●	C	D	E		43	A	B	C	●	E
19	A	B	●	D	E		44	A	B	C	●	E
20	A	B	C	D	●		45	A	●	C	D	E
21	A	B	●	D	E		46	A	B	C	●	E
22	A	●	C	D	E		47	●	B	C	D	E
23	A	B	●	D	E		48	A	B	●	D	E
24	A	B	C	●	E		49	A	●	C	D	E
25	A	●	C	D	E		50	A	B	C	●	E

Test 4 - Verbal Reasoning

#	A	B	C		#	A	B	C
1	●	B	C		26	A	B	●
2	A	●	C		27	●	B	C
3	A	●	C		28	A	●	C
4	●	B	C		29	●	B	C
5	A	●	C		30	●	B	C
6	●	B	C		31	A	●	C
7	●	B	C		32	A	B	●
8	A	B	●		33	A	●	C
9	A	●	C		34	●	B	C
10	A	●	C		35	A	B	●
11	●	B	C		36	A	●	C
12	A	B	●		37	A	B	●
13	A	●	C		38	A	●	C
14	●	B	C		39	A	B	●
15	A	●	C		40	●	B	C
16	A	●	C					
17	●	B	C					
18	A	●	C					
19	●	B	C					
20	A	●	C					
21	A	B	●					
22	●	B	C					
23	A	B	●					
24	●	B	C					
25	A	●	C					

Test 5 - Observation and Memory

#	A	B	C		#	A	B	C
1	A	B	●		8	A	B	●
2	A	●	C		9	●	B	C
3	●	B	C		10	A	B	●
4	A	●	C		11	●	B	C
5	●	B	C		12	A	●	C
6	A	●	C		13	●	B	C
7	A	B	●		14	●	B	C

Pass mark = 140 correct answers
N.B. Test 2: one mark per question providing you have filled-in the correct circles ; 0 marks if you have made any errors in checking.